S L I C K

S L I C K

Whitey Ford

with
Phil Pepe

WILLIAM MORROW AND COMPANY, INC.
New York

Library of Congress Cataloging-in-Publication Data

Ford, Whitey, 1928–
　Slick.

　Includes index.
　1. Ford, Whitey, 1928–　.　2. Baseball players—
United States—Biography.　3. New York Yankees (Base-
ball team)　I. Pepe, Phil.　II. Title.
GV865.F613A3　1987　　796.357′092′4 [B]　　87-1615
ISBN 0-688-06690-9

Printed in the United States of America

First Edition

1 2 3 4 5 6 7 8 9 10

BOOK DESIGN BY DALE COTTON

To Joan—my best fan, my best friend, my wife

PREFACE

The Ol' Perfesser, Casey Stengel, used to have a favorite expression that he used when he thought some of his players were getting a little too big for their britches and needed some toning down. He used to call us "whiskey slick." I think Whitey, Billy, and I heard that expression more than anybody. After a while, Billy and I picked up on it and we began to call Whitey "Slick," and the name just stuck.

The nickname just seemed to fit Whitey perfectly, for so many reasons. He was a city slicker. He was slick on the mound, outsmarting hitters and using every trick in the book and some that aren't. And he liked to have a drink now and again.

To this day, I still call Whitey "Slick." And he calls me "Kid." Whitey calls everybody "Kid."

I remember the first time I met Whitey. Of course I had

heard about him, but I first met him at his wedding. It was in April 1951 and Whitey was on furlough from the army at the time. We had just played an exhibition game against the Dodgers in Brooklyn and Casey insisted that the whole team had to go to Whitey and Joan's wedding. So we all loaded on a bus after the game with the Dodgers and drove over to Donahue's in Queens for the wedding.

I never even went in to the wedding reception. I was too shy in those days. So while the other guys went in, I just stayed on the bus and waited until we were ready to leave. After about an hour, the guys started coming back on the bus, and then Whitey and Joan came on the bus to thank us for coming to the wedding, and Whitey and I shook hands, and that was the first time we met.

It wasn't until after Whitey got out of the army in 1953 that we started hanging around together. The three of us, Whitey, Billy, and me—what an odd trio we were. Me a country kid from Oklahoma. Billy a wise guy from the streets of Berkeley, California. And Whitey, the original city slicker.

At first, I didn't know what to make of Whitey. I had never known anybody like him. It was like he was from another world. He always reminded me of James Cagney, the way he strutted around. Remember the movie when Cagney pushed the grapefruit in the girl's face? To me, that was Whitey Ford. Not that he ever pushed a grapefruit in a girl's face. At least I don't think he ever did.

And the way he spoke! He used to get on me for the way I talked and then I'd go into a bar with him and he would order a "vodker and soder."

I remember one winter when Billy and Whitey came down to Commerce, Oklahoma, to go hunting. Whitey had never been hunting before. He didn't even know how to use a shotgun. I gave him a gun and every time he had to shoot it, he would pump the gun like he saw them do in the movies. But it was an automatic shotgun and he didn't have to pump it. But he kept pumping it. One time, he had the gun pointing right at me and Billy and he started pumping it. It's a good thing he did. If he had pulled the trigger, one of us would have been gone.

I took them to south Texas, to the hill country, to hunt for deer. We made the trip in an old Model A Ford, the kind with the rumble seat. I was in the passenger seat and Billy was driving and Whitey was in the back, in the rumble seat. All of a sudden we saw a deer and Whitey put his gun right between me and Billy, right next to my ear, and he fired at the deer. The shot must have broken my eardrum because my ear still whistles every once in a while.

As a pitcher, Whitey was the best. The Chairman of the Board. I've often said if I was choosing up sides to pick a team, with every player in the major leagues to choose from, if I had the first pick, I would take Whitey. After all, they say pitching is 90 percent of the game, and there's no pitcher I would rather have on my team.

I know I'll get some arguments there from people who say Sandy Koufax was the greatest pitcher of his day or Bob Gibson or Warren Spahn. But Whitey won seven out of every ten decisions, didn't he? And nobody in the history of baseball has ever done better than that.

The amazing thing about Whitey was that he was always the same after a game, win or lose. If I had a bad day, I wouldn't want to talk to anybody. If he lost a tough game, he'd still sit there in front of his locker and answer all the writers' questions. I couldn't do it and I couldn't understand how he could. And it wasn't because he didn't care, because in addition to being the best pitcher I ever saw, he was also the greatest competitor.

I remember one game in 1956, either the last game of the season or the next-to-last. Anyway, we were playing the Baltimore Orioles and it was Whitey's last start of the season. He had nineteen wins and he had never won twenty games in his career, and I knew how badly he wanted to win this game. I wanted to win for him just as badly.

The Orioles started a young kid named Charlie Beamon and he beat us, 1–0. The only run scored when I dropped a fly ball. I wanted to crawl all the way back to Oklahoma. I didn't have the heart to face Whitey after the game, knowing I had cost him a chance to win twenty for the first time in his career.

I was almost in tears. I dreaded the thought of facing Whitey. But he made it easy for me. He came up to me in the clubhouse, put his hand on my shoulder, and said, "Forget it, Mick. Let's have a beer!"

That's the kind of guy Whitey Ford is.

After Billy Martin was traded in 1957, it was just Whitey and me. We used to get adjoining rooms on the road and we always went out together. We did that until I retired after the 1968 season. I probably have spent more time with Whitey than with any other person on earth. I know Whitey better than I know my own brothers. I've spent more time with Whitey than I have with them.

I've known Whitey almost forty years now and I never once remember having an argument or a disagreement with him. In fact, I can't remember Whitey ever having an argument with anybody. There isn't anybody that I know of who knows him and doesn't like him. That's just the kind of guy he is. He's also the best family man I know. He's totally involved with the lives of each of his three children and he's devoted to Joan and his mother and Joan's mother and his grandchildren. I know when Whitey's three kids were growing up and we were on the road, he'd always be on the telephone with each of them, staying involved in what was important to them.

Don't get me wrong: Whitey can get tough if he has to. But he never has to. He just has a way about him, a way of talking to people that makes them like him.

I know men are not supposed to talk about love for other men, especially so-called macho athletes. But I don't mind telling you that I love Whitey Ford. I couldn't love him more if he was my own brother.

—MICKEY MANTLE
Dallas, November 1986

SLICK

PROLOGUE

It was one of those bitter January days in New York, the kind of day that was too cold to snow. It was one of those days that makes you happy to be inside, comfortable and warm, with nothing to do, nowhere to go. It was a lazy day on Long Island's North Shore. Tuesday, January 15, 1974.

I had agreed that winter to return to the New York Yankees as their pitching coach for the 1974 season, and I was looking forward to it. Yankee Stadium was being renovated, and the Yankees had worked out a deal with the City of New York to play their games for the 1974 and 1975 seasons as co-tenants with the New York Mets in Shea Stadium in Flushing, Queens, which was only about ten miles from my home.

This was going to be the start of a new era for the Yankees.

Prologue

They were under new ownership. George M. Steinbrenner III, a shipbuilder from Cleveland, had bought the team from the Columbia Broadcasting System just a year before and he had impressed me with his drive and his enthusiasm. George was the main reason I was coming back as a coach after being out of baseball for six years.

It was still six weeks before I had to report to the Yankees' spring training camp in Fort Lauderdale, Florida, so I was just hanging around most of the winter, doing as little as possible.

The kids were grown up, Sally Ann working for American Airlines and the boys in college. It was just me and Joan in that big house in Lake Success, New York. I had recently bought myself a new toy, a pool table, and after dinner that Tuesday evening, I was shooting some pool when the telephone rang. Joan answered it and came back and told me Jack Lang was on the line.

At the time, Lang was a baseball writer for the *Long Island Press,* a newspaper that is no longer publishing. He regularly covered the Mets and I thought it was strange that he would be calling me, especially in January. I had forgotten for the moment that Jack was also the secretary-treasurer of the Baseball Writers Association of America.

I picked up the telephone and heard Jack talking on the other end. The next few moments are a blur in my mind, but to the best of my recollection, this is what I remember Jack saying:

"Congratulations, Slick. You've been elected to the Hall of Fame."

I was in a complete state of shock. I dropped the pool cue and started crying. I told Joan the news and she started crying. The two of us, standing there and bawling like a couple of babies. It must have been five minutes before I was able to compose myself and talk to Lang.

"Can you be at the Americana Hotel tomorrow morning at ten?" Lang said.

"Hell, yeah," I practically screamed into the phone.

The whole thing had just sort of sneaked up on me. I wasn't even aware that the vote was being taken at that time, although I should have been. The year before, it was different. I had been aware when the vote was being taken because that was my first year of eligibility and there was a lot of speculation in the newspapers about my chances of making it in my first try. Writers kept calling me in the days before the vote was to be announced to ask me if I thought I would make it, so I couldn't help noticing when the announcement was due.

I didn't make it my first year and, frankly, I never expected to. In order to be elected, a player has to be named on 75 percent of the ballots cast. In my first year, 284 votes were needed. I got 255.

Warren Spahn was the only one who made it in 1973. I wasn't terribly disappointed because I had heard how difficult it was to be elected in your first year. Joe DiMaggio didn't make it in his first year of eligibility, and if he didn't make it, I figured what chance did I have? I had come close. There was still plenty of time to make it. And I figured my time would come.

After I missed by those twenty-nine votes the first time, I just put it out of my mind. I never thought I had a chance in the second year either, because I had seen so many players miss by thirty or forty votes in their first try, then the next year they missed by twenty or twenty-five votes, and it would take them about three or four years before they finally got in. Besides, my second year of eligibility was Mickey Mantle's first, and I thought he would make it by such a landslide, it would hurt everybody else's chances. As it turned out, I may have gotten in on Mickey's coattails, as the politicians say.

Prologue

I didn't care how it happened, or why. All I knew was that I was thrilled when Jack Lang told me I had made it along with Mickey. For us to get in at the same time, as close as we were, after all we had been through together . . . well, that just made it that much more special.

The next day was the longest of my life. I didn't sleep at all the night before, I was so excited. I left home early in the morning and Mickey and I got together before we had to go downstairs to the Grand Ballroom for the announcement and to meet the press.

Our friend Toots Shor, the noted restaurateur, was waiting there already, holding the Bloody Marys for Mickey and me.

After the announcement and the press conference, Commissioner Bowie Kuhn took us to lunch at the "21" Club. We had to pass Toots's place and Rose's, a restaurant next to Toots's where I had spent some time and had consumed some booze. About a dozen guys who hung out at Rose's, guys I had had a few drinks with over the years, were outside Rose's waiting for us, and they came out to greet us. That really made me feel good.

We finished lunch at about three and we went back to Rose's for a few drinks with the guys. It was about 6 P.M. when we found out the New York Press Photographers were having their annual dinner at Shea Stadium, so we decided to continue our partying there. Toots had recently broken his hip in a fall and he was in a wheelchair, but we all got into a limousine and drove out to Shea for the photographers' party. We didn't leave there until 2 A.M., and we had been on the go since early in the morning.

Being elected to the Hall of Fame is, without a doubt, the highlight of my career. But it never was anything I imagined was possible, or anything I dared dream about when I was a kid growing up on the sidewalks of New York.

Prologue

Most kids dream about growing up and becoming a major league baseball player. I dreamed, too, but I never really thought I would make it because as a kid I always was too small. In fact, it wasn't until my third year in the minor leagues that I even began to think I had a chance to make the majors.

CHAPTER 1

If you ask me for my earliest recollection, I'd have to say it was a big brick building on Sixty-sixth Street and Second Avenue in Manhattan. Now it's an apartment house, but back when I remember it, the building was where they parked the trolley cars at night. I vaguely remember throwing a rubber ball against that building when I was just a kid, which is also my first recollection of any ball playing.

I had to be about four years old at the time, because by the time I was five, we had moved across the river to Queens.

For the record, though, I was born on October 21, 1928, on Sixty-sixth Street in Manhattan, about a hundred city blocks and one body of water south of Yankee Stadium.

I can hardly remember living in Manhattan, but my years growing up in Astoria, Queens, are not only vivid, they bring back pleasant memories. I was born during the Depression, so I guess we didn't have much money, but it's funny because I never thought of myself as poor. I was an only child and both my parents worked, so there was always enough money for food and clothing and even for the little luxuries, like going to the movies or going up to Yankee Stadium for a baseball game.

My dad worked for Consolidated Edison and later, after I was playing ball professionally, he and a friend, Jack Rogers, bought the Ivy Room, a bar in Astoria.

Mom always worked when I was a kid. I remember her working as a bookkeeper for the A&P on Fifty-third Street and Second Avenue in Manhattan. Later she worked for the Equitable Life Insurance Company.

We lived on Thirty-fourth Avenue in Astoria, an area that was typical of Queens in those days, sort of Archie Bunker country. Our neighborhood was made up mostly of second-generation families, a mixture of Irish, Italian, and Polish. It was predominantly Catholic and the church was the center of much of the social activity there.

The neighborhood was distinguished by three- and four-story apartment buildings, walk-ups, and some one- and two-family houses. Among the landmarks were the Ronzoni macaroni factory and the Con Ed building.

It was a very close-knit community, kind of like one big family. We would spend a lot of time on the front stoop of each other's houses. They had a big block party for me the year I was called up by the Yankees. There was a big sign they put up across the street, WELCOME EDDIE FORD, OUR HOMETOWN HERO, TO THE YANKEES. The whole neighborhood came out. Everybody had a barrel of beer on their stoop. They had a band and dancing in the street. It was very nice.

I didn't need much as a kid. All my entertainment was right

there on the streets of Astoria. We played stickball in the summer, football in the fall, and roller hockey in the winter. You didn't need a calendar to tell what season of the year it was in Astoria. As soon as the fall rolled around, the stickball bats and rubber Spalding balls would disappear and somebody would bring out a football and start tossing it around.

I played stickball before I was old enough to play baseball. There were very few cars in those days, so we could play our stickball games right in front of our apartments and rarely would we have to stop the game for a car to pass.

I remember playing a lot with my uncles. Rudy and Bob Johnson, my mother's brothers, weren't much older than I was and they would use me as the mascot for the stickball team. I was so proud. What I didn't know was that "mascot" was a nice way of saying "gopher." When the ball was hit on the roof, it was my job to retrieve it.

My father, Jim Ford, was a pretty good baseball player himself. He never got a chance to play pro ball, but he gained a reputation in our neighborhood as a ballplayer by playing with the Con Ed baseball team.

I don't remember my dad being very interested in baseball as a fan until after I signed with the Yankees. Then he followed my career very closely. Every summer, he and my mom would take a one-week vacation and spend it wherever I was playing in the minor leagues, watching me play.

I lived in a very sports-minded neighborhood. The Cuccinello brothers, Tony and Al, lived only a few blocks away. I didn't know them then, but I'd heard about them because Tony played in the major leagues for the Brooklyn Dodgers, New York Giants, and Boston Braves, among others, and Al had had a cup of coffee with the Giants. Later, Tony and Al both played for the Bushwicks, a well-known semipro team of the day. The Bushwicks had several former major leaguers and were better than most minor league teams.

The big hero of our neighborhood was Sam Mele, who was a hotshot baseball and basketball star at New York University. I remember my father taking me to a gym on Steinway Street in Astoria to watch Sam play basketball. Then, of course, Sam got to be a local celebrity when he signed a contract with the Boston Red Sox. I didn't know Sam very well in those days, but after I joined the Yankees I pitched against him and we got to be good friends.

Another kid in the neighborhood was Anthony Benedetto. He was a few years older than me, so he was not part of my crowd, and he wasn't too interested in sports. His family owned a beauty salon on Thirty-fourth Street and Anthony worked in the salon, but he was more interested in becoming a singer than he was in being a hairdresser. He would work little clubs in the area, or he would sing at weddings and parties. He stuck with it and Anthony Benedetto, who changed his name to Tony Bennett, reached his goal and became a singer.

Through the years, kids have asked me how they could prepare to be a major league baseball player. Everybody is different, but I believe what helped me most was that when I was a kid, we used to play baseball all the time, weather permitting, of course.

There was an outdoor arena in our neighborhood, on Northern Boulevard and Forty-third Street, called the Madison Square Garden Bowl, and they used to hold fights there during the summer. Joe Louis fought there and so did Barney Ross and Henry Armstrong. On either side of the Bowl there were baseball fields, about six or eight of them, and you could always go there and be sure you'd have a field to play on.

I spent most of my time on those fields. When school was

in session, we'd get to the field at about 3:15 and play until it got dark. On Saturday and Sunday, and during the summer, we'd be on those fields all day long, six, eight, ten hours every day.

As a result, there must have been times I came to bat two hundred times a week. If you were a pitcher, you might have to throw a couple of hundred pitches in a week.

Nowadays, with organized Little Leagues, you might play two games a week and a kid is lucky if he gets to bat six times a week. That's the difference. There's no comparison. We learned how to play by playing.

As far back as I can remember, I rooted for the Yankees. I guess there were two reasons why I was a Yankee fan. One was that they were winning all the time and kids are natural front-runners. Another is that my uncles were Yankee fans and they used to take me to Yankee Stadium. Make it three reasons. The third was Joe DiMaggio. I took a liking to him and he became my favorite player.

I remember every morning my father would buy the *Daily News* for two cents, and the first thing I would do was turn to the sports section and look at the box score to see how many hits DiMaggio had gotten.

In school, we used to have this betting pool where you would get six-to-one odds on three players getting six hits. I'd put up a penny and every day I would take DiMaggio and Ted Williams and somebody else. Of course, it was a sucker bet because it's hard to pick three players who will get six hits. It was especially hard if you picked Ted Williams because since he walked so much, he might have only two official at bats in a game.

The best time for me was when my uncles would take me up to Yankee Stadium. We'd ride the subway from Astoria all the way up to the Bronx for only a nickel. And we'd sit on the bleachers, where the tickets cost 25 cents. So for 35 cents and maybe another quarter for a hot dog and a Coke, we'd have great entertainment.

The first and only time I ever asked a major league player for an autograph was when I saw a bunch of kids following two guys up a hill toward the Concourse Plaza Hotel, and I decided to tag along. Everybody was handing them pieces of paper and getting autographs, so I decided to do the same thing. I got a piece of paper from somewhere and shoved it in front of these guys and they signed it.

I didn't even know who they were until I looked at their names on the paper. They were Pinky Higgins and Jim Tabor, who played for the Boston Red Sox.

I don't know what I ever did with those autographs. I guess the same thing happened to them that has happened to most of the ones I have signed through the years. I must have signed tens of thousands of autographs in my life and never have I walked into a house and had someone say, "Here's your autograph. I've been saving it all these years." But in recent years, many collectors have sprung up and autograph and collectors' shows have become big business. I would say I average about five or six shows a year myself.

Even though my uncles were big Yankees fans, their mother, my Grandma Johnson, was a Giants fan. She had come to this country from Sweden, but for some reason she got hooked on baseball. She used to listen to the ball games on the radio all the time and she probably knew as much about baseball as anyone in my family. She rooted for the Giants until Leo Durocher left Brooklyn and went to manage the Giants. Then she switched to rooting for the Dodgers. She didn't like Durocher; she thought he was a ruffian. She liked Burt Shotton, who replaced Leo as manager of the Dodgers. Grandma Johnson thought Shotton was a kind gentleman, which is exactly how he looked sitting in the dugout in his street clothes and straw hat. Grandma Johnson rooted for the Dodgers until I got to the Yankees, then she switched. I think she did it reluctantly.

Grandma Johnson had a job working for the Harper brothers. They owned *Harper's Bazaar* magazine, and Grandma Johnson was their cleaning woman, but actually she was more than that. She was the caretaker for the Harpers' big house on Lexington Avenue and Thirty-eighth Street. The house is still there, but it's more of a museum now.

Henry Harper lived in the house. It had fifteen rooms and seven fireplaces, and every September, just before school started, Grandma Johnson would arrange for me to go up to the house on Lexington and spend a week polishing the seven brass fireplaces. For this, I got paid $3.

I had a lot of other jobs through the years, during the summer and later, in the winter, when I would come back from playing in the minor leagues. I worked for Railway Express and for Equitable Life Insurance, but I guess I'll always remember polishing those brass fireplaces for $3, because that was the first money I earned.

When I was about seventeen, the Forans moved into the neighborhood, right across the street from us. Joe Foran had been a pretty good soccer player in Dublin, Ireland. He was good enough for some team from the Bronx to pay his way over to this country to play for them. They got him a job as a carpenter, but he was really getting paid to play soccer. He couldn't hit a nail in a piece of wood at the time, although he ended up actually becoming a very good carpenter.

After a few years in the Bronx, Joe Foran decided to move

his family to the suburbs, which is how they ended up in Astoria.

The Forans had three daughters. The middle one, Joan, was a pretty thing, but I didn't pay much attention to her at first because she was three years younger than me and I was more interested in playing ball than I was in girls back then. I never dreamed at the time that I would end up marrying her.

I remember a lot about the old neighborhood. I learned how to play ball there. I also learned how to drink beer.

There used to be a couple of old men in the neighborhood, not bums, but hangers-on. When we were about sixteen and still too young to drink, four of us would chip in 10 cents apiece and get one of these old men to buy us a container of beer. The container cost 30 cents, so he'd buy one for us and he'd have 10 cents left over to buy himself a beer. We got our container and he got his beer, so everybody was happy. We'd take our container to Kelly's Park and sit around drinking and talking. We'd get about eight beers out of the container, two apiece.

Every once in a while I still have reason to go back to the old neighborhood for something and it's amazing that it has hardly changed at all. Probably the biggest change is that the old Madison Square Garden Bowl is gone and there's a post office and a United States Steel building in its place. But the apartment houses and the retail stores are just about like they were forty to forty-five years ago. The only difference is that when I was a kid there were a lot of vacant lots for us to play in and now there are buildings and factories where the lots used to be.

I guess it was a pretty tough neighborhood. I don't remember any gangs, but there were occasional street fights and you had to learn how to take care of yourself. I didn't get involved in much of that. I was too busy playing ball.

I was thirteen when I first played organized baseball. Until then, we kids would just choose up sides and play. But our fathers got together and bought us uniforms, the first uniform I ever had. We called ourselves the Thirty-fourth Avenue Boys. We stayed together as a team for five years.

By the time I was ready to go to high school, I was a pretty good baseball player and I wanted to play high school ball. But the local school, Bryant High, didn't have a baseball team at the time, so another kid from the Thirty-fourth Avenue Boys, Johnny Martin, and I took the test for Manhattan School of Aviation Trades because it had a baseball team. We passed the test and were accepted at Manhattan Aviation.

For a number of reasons, Manhattan Aviation was the wrong place for me to go to high school. The school was in Manhattan, between Second and Third Avenues on Sixty-second Street, and I lived in Queens, so it meant traveling into the city and back by bus every day, a trip that took about an hour each way. Also, this was a vocational school, which meant that the curriculum did not prepare us for college. Worst of all, the teams we played baseball against were other vocational schools, so the competition was not as good as at the academic schools.

There really was no earthly reason for me to be at Manhattan Aviation, but I was there and I figured I had to make the best of it. The easiest way to describe the school is to compare it to the one in the movie *The Blackboard Jungle*. Manhattan Aviation was exactly like that.

The student body was a mixture of whites, blacks, and Hispanics, a true melting pot. The school was housed in two buildings, which were as old and as dilapidated as you can imagine. In one building, you did schoolwork. In the other, you did shop work.

The idea was that Manhattan Aviation was supposed to

prepare you to become an airplane mechanic, but I had not even the remotest intention of being an airplane mechanic and I don't know anybody who went to school with me who did become one.

The only plane they had was an old-fashioned Piper Cub. It took me three years to make a wing tip. The first year, you made the ribs, which make up the wooden thing inside, and the spar. The second year you made the fitting. The third year, you put a cloth coating on and you painted it over and over—it seemed like about fifty coats of paint—and you had a wing tip. That was all you accomplished after three years of high school. It was a joke.

I wasn't a good student and I wasn't a very good mechanic. My schoolwork was terrible. You had to be good in shop and I wasn't. I think the only reason I graduated was that I never missed a day of school and one of the reasons I didn't miss school was that I wanted to remain eligible to play baseball.

In addition to all the other disadvantages of playing baseball at Manhattan Aviation—the travel, the lack of top-flight competition—there was the problem of our home playing field. It was the worst field you could imagine, right under the Fifty-ninth Street Bridge, which meant that the sun never hit the field and no grass ever grew on it. Besides that, the winos would sleep under the bridge at night and they'd throw their empty bottles on the field. So before every game, we'd have to go all over the field picking up pieces of glass. How we didn't kill ourselves running on those rocks and that broken glass I'll never know.

Despite these handicaps, we had a decent team at Aviation. I was a first baseman in those days. I was only about five feet nine and 150 pounds, but I could hit. Not much power, but I was a good line-drive hitter. I batted about .350 in my high school career.

SLICK

Our second baseman was Vito Valentinetti. I was the first baseman and Vito was the second baseman and we both wound up pitching in the big leagues. What do you suppose are the odds against that happening? Vito pitched for the Washington Senators, Chicago Cubs, and three other clubs. Today, he pitches batting practice for the Mets and Yankees. We've been friends for a long time and it all started when we played the right side of the infield for Manhattan Aviation's baseball team, forty years and about two hundred pounds ago.

In April of my senior year, I went to a Yankees tryout at the Stadium. They gave us a sandwich and a small container of milk and we got five pitches to hit. I took my five cuts and I never even reached the outfield grass. There must have been two hundred guys at the tryout and the pitchers were so wild you had no idea where the ball was going.

Paul Kirchell, the Yankees scout, was running the tryout, and he watched me during infield practice and asked me if I had ever pitched.

"No," I told him, so he took me off to the side and had me throw a few pitches. Then he showed me how to throw a curveball, but I didn't pitch in a game until later that season.

It was the last week of the high school season and we had run out of pitchers. We had a couple hurt and a couple more who didn't show up, so the coach asked me if I would pitch a couple of innings. I said sure.

I always had good control. If there was one thing I could do, even as a kid, it was throw strikes. It was a knack I had picked up in a game we used to play in the neighborhood. You played it with a broomstick and a Spalding rubber ball, but this was not the game of stickball I talked about before.

Stickball was a game you played in the street, with five or six players in the field. The pitcher would throw the ball to the hitter on a bounce and the hitter would hit the ball and run the bases.

This other game was different—it really didn't even have a name. For those of you who have never played it, it was played in a vacant lot or in a schoolyard and you could play it with only one player on each side. A box was drawn on a wall in chalk to represent the strike zone. One guy would stand up next to the box using the broomstick for a bat, and the other guy would step off sixty feet, six inches, and throw the rubber ball into the box. If the hitter connected, instead of running bases, singles, doubles, triples, and home runs would be based solely on the distance the ball was hit.

I could hit the box consistently—and I guess that helped me throw strikes with a baseball.

I pitched only that one time for Manhattan Aviation, in my senior year. Ironically, the year after I entered Aviation, our local school, Bryant, finally started a baseball team. I thought about transferring, but decided against it. I figured I might as well finish up where I had started.

In Astoria at the time, there was another ballplayer who was beginning to get a reputation as a good young pitcher. His name was Billy Loes and he became a star pitcher at Bryant. I really didn't know Billy when we were kids because he came from another neighborhood in Astoria and was a year younger than me. But I knew him by reputation.

Manhattan Aviation did play Bryant once, but Billy and I didn't pitch against one another. He didn't pitch that day and I was still a first baseman at the time.

Billy played sandlot ball with the Astoria Cubs, but we never played against them when I was with the Thirty-fourth Avenue Boys. In fact, I didn't pitch against Billy until the 1953 World Series, when I started the fourth game for the Yankees and he started for the Dodgers.

After the high school season, we went right into the season for the Thirty-fourth Avenue Boys. Our best pitchers had passed the age limit, so we needed to find a couple of pitchers. Johnny Martin, who had gone with me to Aviation and was our catcher there, as well as for the Thirty-fourth Avenue Boys, suggested I pitch. He had caught me that one time in high school and thought I did a good enough job. We worked out an arrangement. I would pitch in every other game and play first base the other times. Don Derle would alternate with me, pitching when I played first base and playing first when I pitched.

We played in the Queens-Nassau League and we went undefeated, 36-0. I was 18-0 as a pitcher and Don Derle was 18-0. Then we played a championship game in the Polo Grounds against a team from the Bronx. That was in September 1946. I pitched the game, and after nine innings, it was still scoreless. We didn't have a hit and they had two, but I led off the top of the tenth with a double to left center. Then Derle singled me home and we won the game, 1–0.

With that victory, we won the *Journal-American* sandlot championship and I was presented with the Lou Gehrig Trophy as the game's Most Valuable Player. And how's this for a coincidence? Twenty-four years later, my son Eddie won the same trophy.

After that game, I got a call from the Boston Red Sox. They offered me $1,000 to sign a contract with them. For somebody who never had any thought of being able to play pro ball, that seemed like all the money in the world. Then the Giants offered me $2,000, and the Red Sox upped their offer to $3,000. The Yankees got into the auction with an offer of $5,500. As far as I was concerned, that was it. I would have signed with the Yankees no matter what they offered, but this was the highest offer anyway.

It was all set. Paul Krichell and Harry Hesse came to our

apartment in Astoria with the contract. They were going to take me to see a bunch of Yankee farmhands play against the Bushwicks in a doubleheader. It was kind of a scouting mission for them and a get-acquainted visit for me.

They arrived at the apartment at 11 A.M., and they pulled out the contract and asked me to sign it.

"What's the hurry?" I said. "We have to come back here after the game. I'll sign it then."

They agreed and we went off to the doubleheader. When we got back, my mother said, "The Giants called while you were out. A man who said he was a scout and his name was Jerry Monte. He said he'll give you sixty-five hundred dollars."

Krichell almost shit. I'm sure he thought he was being set up. But I knew nothing about it. I was tickled when I was offered $1,000 and I would have signed with the Yankees no matter what. But Krichell upped his offer to $7,000 and he was furious about it.

That summer, I had a job with Equitable Life. I worked in the mail room and played on their baseball team. They played in the Industrial League against other companies like the Metropolitan Life Insurance Company and the American Can Company. I got paid $37 twice a month and $5 a game.

The Industrial leagues are no longer in existence in the New York area, but at the time, they were very prominent and the competition was quite good.

People have asked me what I would have done with my life if I hadn't become a professional baseball player. I wondered the same thing myself many times.

I might have remained with Equitable in some capacity, but not selling insurance. The reason I say that is when I got out of the army, Al McGuire and I took the test three times and we failed it all three times. So Al went down to Belmont Abbey

College and started his coaching career, and I stuck with baseball. Later I worked with M. Donald Grant at Fahnestock and Company, and I might have had a career with them.

The only thing I regret about my life is that I didn't go to college and get an education, so I consider myself very lucky to have made my living in baseball.

One of the things I remember about working at Equitable is that one day Dixie Walker and Marty Marion came up to our offices. They were two of the biggest stars in the major leagues at the time and the whole building was buzzing because they were there. It turned out the reason for their visit was to talk about a pension fund for major league players. That was one of the early meetings that led to the creation of the Major League Players Association.

My Yankee contract called for me to get $3,500 when I signed and another $3,500 when I reported to spring training. I signed my contract and they presented me with a check for $3,500. My family didn't even have a bank account, so I had to take the check to work at Equitable and get it cashed. They gave it to me in seventy crisp, new $50 bills.

My mother knew I had the money, but she thought I had stashed it somewhere. Little did she know I was carrying it around with me. The next morning, a Saturday, me and my friend Dominick Monzalillo took the subway to Times Square in Manhattan. We were both wearing sneakers and I had on these faded dungarees and my ratty old baseball jacket. Dominick was a tough-looking kid with a swarthy complexion. We walked into Vim's, a combination appliance and sporting-goods store, on Forty-second Street.

I was going to use some of my bonus money to buy a ra-dio/record player for my mother and father. It was on sale for $181 and I was going to surprise them with it.

So we walked into the store and I said to the guy behind the counter, "I want that radio/record player."

"OK," he said. "That will be a hundred and eighty-one dollars."

I put my hand in my pocket and took out my bonus money, seventy $50 bills. I peeled off four of the bills and handed them to the guy behind the counter.

"Just a minute," he said. "I'll wrap your radio."

And he went in the back and was gone for a long time. We must have waited about ten or fifteen minutes. The next thing we knew, two cops were in the store and they came up to me and asked me what I was doing with all that money.

I tried to tell them I had just signed a contract with the New York Yankees and this was my bonus money, but they took one look at me and Dominick and they wouldn't buy it. I had no identification with me, so I had to call my mother.

Yes, my mother told the cops, that was my money. She had no idea I had it with me and she was going to kill me when I got home, but it was mine, all right. Not only was I in trouble with my mother, but my surprise was ruined.

So now the cops were satisfied and they left. And the guy behind the counter had the nerve to say, "OK, fellas, you can have your record player now."

"Get out of here, you son of a bitch," I told the guy. Then we went to another store and bought another record player.

The day I signed with the Yankees, I went to Yankee Stadium. It turned out to be the first game Yogi Berra and Bobby Brown played for the Yankees. They had just been called up from the minor leagues to finish out the 1946 season. It was the first time I met Yogi.

I'll never forget it. I guess it was Paul Krichell who introduced us.

"Larry," he said, "I want you to meet Eddie Ford, who just signed with us. Eddie, this is Larry Berra."

People were still calling him "Larry" then and I wouldn't become "Whitey" until I was in the minor leagues.

It was the great Lefty Gomez, of all people, who stuck me with the name "Whitey." Lefty was managing the Yankees' Binghamton club in the Eastern League, and I was assigned to go to spring training with his team in 1947. They trained at Edenton, N.C., and there were so many players down there, I guess Lefty had a hard time remembering all their names, so he just gave them nicknames. I was "Blondie" or "Whitey" for obvious reasons. Eventually, he settled on "Whitey."

It was years before the name stuck. Even after I joined the Yankees, I was still "Eddie." In my early years, I signed autographs "Eddie Ford."

It wasn't until guys I played with in the minor leagues like Bob Porterfield and Tommy Gorman joined the Yankees that anybody started calling me "Whitey." They love nicknames in professional sports and pretty soon all the players were calling me "Whitey." The writers picked it up and started using it in their stories, and that's how the name stuck. Today, the only people who call me "Eddie" are my mother and my uncles and a few people who knew me when I was a kid. Even my wife, Joan, calls me "Whitey," and we have known each other since we were teenagers.

One of the guys who went to spring training with me was a fellow from the neighborhood, Johnny Simmons. His brother, Connie, was the center for the New York Knickerbockers basketball team in the late forties. Johnny also played in the NBA for one season, 1946–47, with the Boston Celtics. He managed to make the major leagues with the Washington Senators briefly in the 1949 season.

I was glad to have Johnny to run around with because I had only been away from home before twice: a couple of weeks during the summer when I was a kid, and one day when I went to Youngstown, Ohio, for the Industrial League national tournament.

We at Equitable had won the Industrial League in New York, and we went to Youngstown for the national playoffs. It was the first time most of us had ever been away from home on an overnight trip. Instead of sticking with the younger players who won the local championship for them, Equitable went out and got a bunch of ringers from the Bushwicks and the Queens Club, former major and minor leaguers who were playing semipro ball in the area.

So we made the trip to Youngstown, but we never got to play. Instead, they used these ringers and they lost a doubleheader the first day and were eliminated from the tournament. We were packed to stay a week, but we were back after one day, and it was a big disappointment for us because we thought we could have done better than these so-called ringers.

One night in Edenton, Johnny Simmons and another guy named Ray Passapenka and I decided to go to the local carnival. We had a 10:00 P.M. curfew, so when it got to be 9:40, we decided to take one last ride on the Ferris wheel before we went back. We figured the ride would take five minutes and we'd have plenty of time to get back to our rooms.

We got on the Ferris wheel and it went round and round and round. We looked at the clock and it was getting close to ten and we started yelling at the guy running the wheel to stop it and let us off. But he pretended not to hear us and we kept going round and round and round. Finally, he let us off exactly at ten, and we ran like hell back to our hotel, and who should we run into in the lobby but Lefty Gomez and his wife, the former actress June O'Day.

It was our first spring training and we were scared. It was five minutes past ten, which meant we'd missed curfew by five minutes.

"Where have you been?" Gomez said.

We told him the story about the Ferris wheel and he just looked at us and said, "Bullshit. You're fined five dollars each."

About ten years later, I was with the Yankees and Joe DiMaggio had a television show between games of doubleheaders. This one day, he had Lefty Gomez as his guest and I was watching the show on the television set in the players' lounge. Gomez started telling the story about the carnival and the Ferris wheel in Edenton, N.C., and he said, "I saw Ford get on the Ferris wheel one night and I told the guy to keep him on until ten o'clock. I gave the guy a couple of bucks to keep the wheel going, then I walked back to the hotel with my wife and waited in the lobby for my three pigeons to show up."

After the show, Lefty came into the Yankees clubhouse with DiMaggio.

"You son of a bitch," I shouted at him. "How can you keep that from me for ten years?"

Gomez was laughing like hell. "I got a lot of mileage out of that story at banquets."

"Oh, yeah?" I said. "Well, give me back the ten dollars you fined me."

So he reached into his pocket, took out a $10 bill and handed it to me.

I finally got my revenge. He had only fined me $5.

*   *   *

After spring training, I was sent to Butler, Penn., in the Class C Middle Atlantic League for my first year in professional baseball. It was a rather uneventful year. I was paid $250 a month, which was the good part. I was doing what I enjoyed and they were paying me for it. I liked playing in Butler. What I didn't like was the travel, those terrible bus trips. We'd have to go from Butler to Erie, Pa., to Niagara Falls, in this rickety old schoolbus. We'd sit on that bus anywhere from ten to twelve hours. Then, after we played, we'd climb back on the bus for another twelve-hour trip home. We might get in at 7 A.M., then right away have to play a day game.

I still weighed about 150 pounds and stood five nine, but I had a pretty good year. All I had was a curveball and a mediocre fastball, but I could throw the ball over the plate and in class C baseball, that was all you had to do. I was 13-4, but I didn't dazzle anybody and I still didn't think I would ever pitch in the big leagues.

One of my teammates at Butler was Frank Verdi, a tough Italian kid from Brooklyn who had played basketball at Boys High School. I hit it off with him real good and we became roommates.

Frank has spent his entire life in baseball, over forty years, most of them in the minor leagues. I guess he managed in the minors for something like twenty-five years. He managed the Orioles team in Rochester and he was fired after the 1985 season. He was without a job and I kept hounding George Steinbrenner to hire him. Every day I'd send a note to George, "Don't forget Verdi. Don't forget Verdi." George finally hired him as a scout. It was the least I could do for a guy who saved my life.

That happened a few years ago in Fort Lauderdale. Frank

was managing a minor league team in the Yankees' system and Joan and I decided to have a dinner party at our apartment. We invited Frank and his wife, Mike Ferraro and his wife, Yogi Berra and his wife, and Mickey Mantle and his wife.

We were eating chili, and Mickey started telling a funny story about his experiences in the minor leagues. I had some chili in my mouth and I started laughing. We were in the dining room and I knew I couldn't swallow the chili, so I jumped up to run into the kitchen and spit the chili into the sink.

When I got to the kitchen, I passed out. My sons Eddie and Tommy were there, and they found me lying on the kitchen floor. According to them I started to get purple. Mickey got hysterical. Yogi didn't know what to do. Eddie was going to start giving me mouth-to-mouth resuscitation.

Then Frank Verdi came in and hit me right in the chest twice. Eddie was down by my face and he said a little bean popped out of my mouth when Frank hit me. I didn't know any of this because I was unconscious, but the next day my chest hurt so much, I thought I was dead. So Frank saved my life.

One of the things I remember about Butler is that it was only about twenty miles from Pittsburgh, and we used to get the Pirate games on the radio. The Pirates had an announcer named Rosy Rosewell, who was quite a character. Ralph Kiner was with the Pirates and he was hitting a lot of home runs, and every time Kiner hit one, Roswell would shout, "Look out, Aunt Millie, here she comes!" And the next thing you would hear would be the sound of broken glass, as if Kiner's homer had crashed through somebody's window.

Years later, I met Arnold Palmer at Del Miller's "Adios" golf tournament. One night we were talking and I happened to mention that I spent my first year in professional baseball in Butler.

"Hell," he said, "I grew up in Butler."

Arnold's a year younger than me, so he had to be in high school in 1947 when I broke in.

"Jeez," I said, "too bad I didn't know you in those days—I'd have gotten you some tickets for the games."

"Oh, yeah," Arnie said. "Tickets were really hard to get in those days."

We drew about two hundred people on a good day in Butler.

It was a very uneventful year, and even if I didn't exactly knock them dead, my 13-4 record was good enough for them to bring me back for another season. It meant I wouldn't have to look for a job for at least another six months.

I thought my 13-4 record entitled me to a raise, and when I jumped up to Norfolk, a class B league team, I was sure it meant I'd be making more money. I was in for a surprise. Bruce Henry, who later was the Yankees' traveling secretary, was the general manager at Norfolk, and he told me that the owner said I would have to take a cut to $200 a month. It was the only pay cut I ever took in my career. The owner was a man I knew only as Colonel Dawson. "Tomato Face" Dawson, he was called, because of his ruddy complexion, which I always suspected he got not outside in the sun, but indoors under the lights of some saloon. Old Tomato Face was the cheapest guy in the Yankees organization, outside of George Weiss. I was pissed about having to take a cut, but it was either that or find a job.

My manager at Norfolk was Earl Bolyard and my teammates included Hank Foiles and Clint Courtney, both of whom were to catch in the big leagues, and Frank Verdi again. I had a good year at Norfolk. I won sixteen and lost eight, had sixteen complete games, and even led the league in strikeouts with 171. I still didn't throw hard, so I was getting most of my strikeouts with my curveball.

It turned out to be a disappointing season because we didn't make the playoffs and I was counting on that to make up for the pay cut I'd had to take. At least I knew that my 16-8 record would mean a promotion the following year, and a promotion would mean a raise. At least I assumed it would.

Money was tight and when Clint Courtney asked me to go with him to play winter ball in Mexico, the idea appealed to me. The Yankees didn't want me to go, but I said screw them. Where were they when old Tomato Face cut my salary $50 a month? I made $200 a month in Norfolk and the Mazatlán club in Mexico was willing to pay me $400 a month to play winter ball. I didn't see how I could turn it down.

Going to Mexico was a good experience professionally. I got to play against some of the best players I had seen. A lot of triple A players came down from the States, like Charlie Silvera, who later caught for the Yankees. And there were some good native Mexicans in the league, like Felipe Montemayor, who later played with the Pittsburgh Pirates, and Chile Gomez, who had played with Philadelphia and Washington.

Our center fielder was the best player I had ever seen up to that point. His name was Mala Torres. His son Hector later played with Houston and the Cubs, among others. Mala was good enough to play in the major leagues himself. I'm convinced, had he played in the majors, he would have been a star. He was that good. He had offers from a lot of clubs, but he wouldn't come to the United States because he didn't speak English and he didn't want to leave Mexico.

Like I said, the few months in Mexico was a great experience. There was just one big problem. I got so sick with amoebic dysentery that I almost died. It was awful. One of the most frightening experiences of my life. I didn't know what to do.

When I got sick down there, I didn't trust the doctors. So I asked the Mexican players for some home remedies. I heard if you drank blackberry brandy and ate cheese, it would stop the diarrhea. I tried it, but it didn't work. Every time I so much as drank a glass of water, I would wind up on the toilet for twenty minutes.

It got so that my rear end was so sore, I would squat up in bed on my elbows and knees and Clint Courtney would sprinkle baby powder on me to cool off my rear.

Several times I tried to leave town, but the owner of my club wouldn't let me go because the playoffs were about to start and he needed me. The owner alerted everybody in town to keep an eye out for me and if I tried to leave to stop me. It was a very small town and my blond hair was not hard to spot in Mexico, so what chance did I have? Several times I would make it to the airport, but somebody would spot me there and call the owner of my club and he'd come and bring me back.

Before I went to Mexico, I had finally started putting on some weight. From 150, I got up to 172, and I had grown an inch to my present height of five ten. But the dysentery just knocked everything out of me and I wound up losing the 22 or so pounds I had gained and then some. I lost about 40 pounds in Mexico and went all the way down to 130. As soon as the playoffs ended, I flew home. My mother met me at La Guardia Airport. She took one look at me, all skin and bones, and she started crying. She thought I had some incurable disease and that I would be dead in a week.

To make matters worse, I was scheduled to report for spring training in about three weeks. I was in no condition to go through training, but I wasn't going to blow it now. After my first two years, with a combined record of 29-12, I thought I had a chance to jump all the way up to triple A ball.

I was home from Mexico only a couple of weeks when it was time to report to Orangeburg, S.C., to George Selkirk, the manager of the Binghamton farm club in the Eastern League. The reason I was training with Binghamton, which was a class A club, instead of Newark, which was class AAA, was that George Weiss and Paul Krichell got pissed at me for going to Mexico against their wishes. To punish me for disobeying them, they sent me to Binghamton. I didn't care. I didn't think I could pitch in triple A anyway.

So I reported to Orangeburg and as soon as I arrived, I called Selkirk in his room.

"Come on up," he said. "I've been expecting you. I'm looking forward to meeting you."

No doubt he had heard all about this kid Eddie Ford, the left-hander who had won twenty-nine games in his first two years in the organization. I'll never forget the look on his face when I walked into his room. Here I was, 130 pounds of skin and bones, and I could tell by the look on his face that Selkirk was saying, "This is going to be my ace left-hander who had such a good year at Norfolk? What the hell is going on here?"

Spring training started and after about ten days I was pitching in Augusta. I was supposed to be in good shape because I'd been playing all winter, but in the third inning I passed out on the mound. Passed right out in a dead faint.

They rushed me to a local hospital and the Yankees arranged to have me flown to New York and checked into Lenox Hill Hospital. I was still carrying around the amoebic dysentery bug from Mexico. It took them nineteen days to get rid of it.

All I remember about my stay in Lenox Hill was being awakened early every morning and some doctor sticking a proctoscope up my behind. It was the old kind that was stiff and hard and didn't bend. Needless to say, I didn't look forward to waking up every morning. I later found out that they were using me as a guinea pig for all the interns.

I didn't get back to Binghamton until May. A whole month

of the season had gone by. I had put back some of the weight I'd lost in Mexico and was back up to about 155 when I reported, and I kept getting heavier as the season went on.

Despite my physical problems, pitching in Mexico did me a world of good. My curveball improved and I started throwing a straight change that became a very effective pitch for me. And I was getting quicker. I was twenty years old now and I was maturing and getting stronger and that made my fastball better.

I had missed the first six weeks of the season at Binghamton, but I still finished with a 16-5 record. I led the league in earned run average with 1.61 and in strikeouts with 151 in 168 innings. I was starting to strike out six and seven guys a game now, and for the first time I began to think I had a chance to make it to the big leagues.

In the middle of the season, we were in last place, but then we just started to put everything together. We had a pretty good team. Frank Verdi was with me for the third straight year. We had Tommy Gorman and a big, strong home-run hitter named Jim Greengrass, who wound up playing with Cincinnati. It was a good league, with players like Gus Bell, Al Smith, and Harry "Suitcase" Simpson.

On the last day of the season, we swept a doubleheader and finished in fourth place, which meant we were in the playoffs. And we just swept right through; we beat Scranton to get to the finals and then we beat Wilkes-Barre to win the league championship. And that's when I began to think about making the Yankees.

We played the final game in Wilkes-Barre on a Sunday and after the game, Verdi, Gorman, and I jumped in the car and drove all the way to Long Island. We were feeling pretty good. We were Eastern League champions and we each had a check for $223 in our pocket to prove it.

SLICK

* * *

You might have heard some story that I called Stengel when we clinched that minor league championship. But it's not true. The day after we got to New York, a Monday, I called Paul Krichell and asked *him* if they could bring me up to the Yankees for the rest of the season. I'll admit that I had a lot of nerve to ask the Yankees to bring me up.

But I wouldn't have called Stengel. I didn't even know him. Even I wasn't ballsy enough to call Stengel directly. I called Krichell because I knew him. And I *didn't* do it the way they said I did, tell Krichell that if they let me join them I'd guarantee them the pennant. The Yankees were in a life-and-death struggle with the Boston Red Sox for the American League pennant at the time and I can see now why they wouldn't want some twenty-year-old kid from class A hanging around. But the way I figured it, there were still two weeks left in the season and I was right there in New York. I thought I might be able to pitch batting practice or go in as a pinch runner or something.

Krichell was a tough old Dutchman, and he was still pissed off at me for going to Mexico, so he probably wasn't thrilled to hear from me so soon. But he didn't say no right away. He must have talked it over with George Weiss, because he called me back later and said no.

"But," Krichell said, "if you behave yourself, we'll take you to spring training with the Yankees next year."

That pacified me. I spent the winter just hanging around, working out because I wanted to report to spring training in good shape, and counting the days until it was time to go to Florida. I was going to be a Yankee.

CHAPTER 2

My mother and father, Grandma Johnson, and my uncle Bob all came to Grand Central Station to see me off to St. Petersburg, where I was going to join the Yankees for spring training. The train ride took over twenty-four hours. My instructions were to go to the Soreno Hotel when I arrived and check into my room.

As soon as I got there, I was met by a photographer who said he needed a picture of me. He took me outside to the shuffleboard court, and standing there, with the shuffleboard stick in his hands, was Tommy Henrich. I knew him immediately from seeing his picture in the newspaper. The photographer introduced us and asked Tommy if he would kindly pose for a picture with me. He agreed and the photographer snapped away.

The next day, the picture appeared in a New York paper.

There were me and Henrich standing by the shuffleboard court, with Tommy holding the stick. It was the first time I had ever had my picture in a New York newspaper and it's a memorable one. I'm standing next to Tommy Henrich, looking at the camera. It's not just a head-and-shoulders shot, it's full-length. And my fly is open. I guess you can say my Yankee debut was an auspicious one.

The Soreno Hotel, even then, was an old, ornate, and stately hotel with fancy chandeliers and violin players in the lobby. The average age of the guests was deceased, and the rules of the house included wearing jackets and ties to the dining room.

Ballplayers didn't get meal money in those days. You took your meals in the hotel dining room or you paid for them yourself. All you had to do was sign the check and leave a tip, a quarter for breakfast, a half dollar for dinner. We had lunch at the field. In addition, each player got $20 a week for his laundry and incidentals.

The first night I was there I roomed by myself because my roommate hadn't arrived yet. I had packed everything I owned because I was going to be away possibly for the entire summer. Everything I owned meant I needed four hangers. I had one suit, two sports jackets, and three pairs of slacks. That was it. My entire wardrobe.

The next night, there was a knock on the door and the door opened and in came this big, smiling, happy guy, and in a big, booming voice he said, "Roomie. So you're Eddie Ford."

His name was Dick Wakefield and he was one of the first big bonus babies in baseball. The Detroit Tigers had given him $52,000 to sign, which at the time was a fortune. He was a big left-handed hitter with tremendous natural ability, and the writers and scouts kept comparing him to Ted Williams, which wasn't fair to Wakefield. He could never live up to the comparison. As a result, his major league career was a dis-appointment. Not to Dick. He didn't seem to mind. He was just a big, friendly, happy-go-lucky guy, which may be one reason he never made it big.

Wakefield came into the room, followed by three bellhops carrying his luggage. He took up about 95 percent of the space in the closet. There he was with dozens of suits, slacks, sports jackets, and sweaters, and there I was with everything I owned on four hangers. Until the day he died, every time I saw Dick after that, he'd always kid me and laugh about my wardrobe.

I was fortunate to have Wakefield for a roommate in my first spring training. Not only was he a major league veteran who knew his way around and could show me the ropes, he helped me get rid of the butterflies that were in my stomach over the fact that I was in camp with the Yankees for the first time.

I was also fortunate that the first person I met when I arrived at the hotel was Tommy Henrich. He didn't know me from a hole in the wall. I'm sure he had never even heard of me, but he made me feel so comfortable.

It wasn't until the next day, when I reported to Miller Huggins Field, that I saw Casey Stengel for the first time. When I walked into the Yankees' clubhouse at Huggins Field, I was a little shocked and disappointed. I figured it would be something like the clubhouse in Yankee Stadium: these huge, spacious lockers, carpeting on the floor, a trainer's room, a players' lounge. After all, this was the major leagues. But it wasn't anything like that. The clubhouses in Norfolk and Binghamton were better. This clubhouse was a piece of shit.

It was one room that was hardly big enough to accommodate the fifty guys crowded into it. The lockers were small and they had just a couple of nails hammered into the wood, and you had to hang your clothes on the nails.

They didn't have twenty coaches and special instructors like they do now. There was Stengel and his three coaches. That was it. There was Jim Turner, the pitching coach; Bill Dickey, who coached the hitters and catchers and was on the lines at first; and Frank Crosetti, who was the infield coach and third-base coach.

The room was crowded and I was scared to death just being there. I was too scared to even talk to anybody. I looked around the room and I could see some familiar faces, veteran players like Henrich, and Johnny Lindell, Cliff Mapes, Gene Woodling, and Ralph Houk. I recognized Yogi Berra because I had met him the day I signed my contract, and I recognized Charlie Silvera from playing against him in Mexico.

Pete Sheehy, the clubhouse man, had all the veteran players on one side of the room, and you could tell how much status each player had by the size of his locker and where it was placed. All the rookies were in the back of the room. I met Billy Martin for the first time, but I can't remember anything special that he said or did. The hotshot rookie in camp in the spring of 1950 was Jackie Jensen, the famed "Golden Boy." He had been a Rose Bowl hero from the University of California and he drove in from California in his big convertible. Jensen never liked to fly, which is one reason his major league career was cut short. Jim Brideweser, an infielder, and an outfielder named Hank Workman were a couple of the other rookies, and we introduced ourselves and went about our business.

I was in the room about fifteen minutes when the door flew open and in walked Joe DiMaggio, all dressed up in a suit and tie. I had never seen a suit that good in my life. He looked so dapper. I'm sure I remained with my mouth open staring at him. I just kept looking over at him and if Joe happened to turn and look in my direction, I'd turn around so he wouldn't catch me staring at him.

The first thing DiMag did when he came in every morning was yell out to Pete Sheehy, "Half a cup of coffee, Petey boy."

Then he'd sit in front of his locker, sipping his coffee and talking with the veteran players, like Lindell, Mapes, Henrich, and Joe Page. I never saw him talking to any rookies, except Billy, but that was because Billy started the conversation. Billy was so outgoing, by the time spring training was over, he was not only talking to Joe like he was DiMag's equal, he was hanging out with him.

I don't think I said a word to Joe all spring. I was so nervous, I wasn't about to go over to him and introduce myself. I was afraid if I did, I'd get so tongue-tied I was liable to forget my own name.

One day I was shagging fly balls in the outfield and Eddie Lopat came over and started talking to me about pitching. He was a veteran pitcher and he was left-handed, too, and we were both from New York, so I guess he just thought he'd take it upon himself to give me some pitching tips. Our pitching styles were kind of similar, so I guess Eddie figured he could be of some help to me.

I really learned a lot from Eddie. In the minors we never worried much about how to pitch to hitters, but now Lopat was telling me things about pitching.

"You're going to see many of the same hitters year after year now," he said. "You're going to have to find out how to get them out. But hitters change and you have to learn to change with them. You might get a guy out with a high fastball one year, but the next year he may start hitting that pitch and you have to switch on him. Move the ball around. High. Low. Inside. Outside.

"You have to get a book on these hitters. How to pitch to them. Are they low-ball hitters or high-ball hitters? Who's looking for the curveball all the time? Who's a first-ball hitter?"

Eddie was putting all that in my head, things I'd never even thought about before. In my three years in the minor leagues I never had anything even resembling a pitching coach. None of my managers had been pitchers. Now I had Jim Turner, who was great with mechanics, and Eddie Lopat, helping me learn how to think out on the mound. I learned more in one spring than I had in three seasons in the minor leagues. But the more I learned, the more I realized I had so much more to learn, and I began to think that maybe I wasn't ready to pitch in the big leagues, after all.

We had been in spring training a couple of weeks and we were scheduled to play an exhibition game in Miami. Some of the guys decided to go on a fishing expedition and they invited me to go with them. The only fishing I had ever done was by dropping a line in the East River off Steinway Street in Astoria, but I thought this might be fun.

There were four of us, Joe DiMaggio, Joe Page, George Stirnweiss, and me. They had rented a fishing boat that took us out into the Atlantic Ocean.

Page was strapped in his seat, trolling, but nobody was catching anything, so he went below and fell asleep, leaving his line in the water. So Stirnweiss pulled Page's line in and took a water bucket and tied it to Page's line.

When a bucket fills up with water, it gets heavy and there's a drag on the line, the same as if a big fish had been hooked. Stirnweiss ran down and woke up Page, shouting, "Joe, Joe, get up, you got one! You got a bite!"

Page came up and took his line and the captain, steering the boat, was in on the gag. Joe started reeling in his line and each time, just as he was about to bring up his "fish," the captain sped up the boat, making it tougher for Page to land his catch. Joe would then lose ground and the line would go out again.

After about a half hour of this, Page was exhausted. Finally, he got his catch close to the boat.

"I got it, I got it!" he shouted.

By this time, all he could see was a big opening in the water, which, of course, was the mouth of the bucket. But Page thought it was the mouth of a fish.

"Look at the mouth on that son of a bitch!" Page shouted. "It's a whopper!"

When he finally pulled it in and saw the bucket, Page was really pissed. But he still didn't know who did it, and nobody was taking credit for the prank.

The next day, back in St. Petersburg, we were in the club-house and Stirnweiss got a broom handle and a bucket and went running through the clubhouse shouting, "Anybody want to go bucket fishing?"

Page chased him all over the clubhouse.

Another time, we went fishing with Ralph Houk. Ralph had a boat and he loved to fish. He used to like to go into the bay to fish for salt-water trout.

One day, Houk, Gene Woodling, and I went out and I was in the middle of the boat, Woodling in the back, and Houk up front. In the center of the boat there was a little pool of water where you would put the fish you caught to keep them fresh.

Right away, we caught three fair-size trout, which we put in the pool. Houk was all excited because it looked like it was going to be a good day and we were going to come home with a big catch. Then we went twenty minutes without a bite and I could see Houk was getting irritable and restless. He was the big fisherman and he was getting nothing.

That gave me an idea. I looked at Woodling and winked, and I whispered for him to give me his line. Houk couldn't see any of this because he was up front and was looking straight ahead, but you could see the smoke coming out of his ears.

Houk wasn't watching and I took one of the fish we had already caught. I hooked it onto Woodling's line and we lowered it back into the water. Now Woodling started fighting like he'd gotten a fish and Houk heard all the fuss and turned around just in time to see Woodling bringing in another trout.

"Great," Houk said, all excited. "They're starting to bite again."

I took another fish out. I put it on my line and then hauled it in. Meanwhile, Houk was going crazy because Woodling and I were landing all the fish and he still hadn't had a bite. And he was supposed to be the great fisherman. You could tell he was frustrated, even embarrassed, because we were catching all the fish and he was getting nothing.

We decided to call it a day and we got back to the dock and Houk said, "OK, start handing me all those fish."

So we handed him the three fish we had caught early and that was it and Houk could see that each fish had about a dozen holes in its mouth where we kept hooking it over and over.

"You son of a bitch," Houk started screaming at Woodling. He began chasing Woodling and me down the dock. I'm sure if he had caught us, he would have killed us.

I was in training camp about two weeks before Casey Stengel even talked to me. I mean directly to me. I had heard him, of course, in clubhouse meetings.

One day, he saw me in the lobby of the hotel and he began talking to me, never calling me by name. I had pitched three good innings against the Phillies in Clearwater and apparently made a good impression on him because Casey started blurting out something about the team needing a fifth starting pitcher and that everybody has an equal chance to make the club and if I really bear down and work hard, I could go north with the team.

Casey had this unusual way of expressing himself. I didn't think he was goofy. Most of what he said made sense. I always saw him talking to the writers. He loved to talk to them and they loved to listen. He would sit in the bar of the Soreno Hotel and the writers always knew they could find him there in case they needed to ask him something. I know he stayed up late because every night when I went to my room, if I happened to look in the bar, Stengel was always sitting there, talking to somebody.

Players were never allowed in the hotel bar. That was a rule Casey had for as long as I played for him.

"Don't drink in the hotel bar," he used to say, "because that's where I do my drinking."

He didn't want to see what the players were doing and he didn't want them to see what he was doing, and I think that makes a lot of sense. I know it avoided a lot of problems.

A few days after Casey talked to me, I pitched against the Tigers in Lakeland and I really took my lumps. My elbow was bothering me at the time, but I wouldn't dare ask out of the game. Instead, I pitched and got knocked around, and a few days later I was sent down to Kansas City. I didn't feel too bad because Tommy Gorman, Hank Workman, and a first baseman named Fenton Mole were also sent down at the same time, and I had thought those guys were going to make the club.

I finished up spring training with the Kansas City club and

then we broke camp and went home to open the season. Our manager was Joe Kuhel, who had played for the Washington Senators and Chicago White Sox. In our first clubhouse meeting on opening day, Joe said: "Fellas, this is the centennial anniversary of Kansas City. So let's win one hundred games this season, one for every year this town has been in existence."

The Kansas City club didn't win one hundred games that year. In fact, on the final day of the season, they lost a doubleheader and that gave them exactly one hundred defeats. I say "they" because I wasn't with the team by then.

I left Kansas City on July 2. We had come off a road trip, arriving in Kansas City from Minneapolis by train. It was 10 A.M. and Parke Carroll, who was running the Kansas City club, called me and told me the Yankees wanted me to report right away.

My instructions were to call the Yankees office as soon as I got home to Astoria. I did and Red Patterson, the Yankees' public relations director, was waiting for my call. He told me to meet him at Grand Central Station. We were going to take a train up to Boston, where I would join the Yankees for the first time.

My record at Kansas City was 6-3, but I had eight complete games in twelve starts and evidently the Yankees thought I was ready to help them.

Patterson and I took the overnight train to Boston, arriving at seven o'clock in the morning. We went right to the Kenmore Hotel, where the team was staying.

The one guy I knew best on the Yankees was Billy Martin. I knew him not only from spring training, but from two weeks he had spent with us in Kansas City earlier that season. The

Yankees sent him down because he wasn't playing much in New York and they wanted him to get in some playing time. It was only for two weeks, but Billy never stopped bitching the whole time. He bitched about the team, about the clubhouse, about the condition of the infield, about the travel. He couldn't wait to get back to New York where he figured he belonged.

So the first thing I did when I arrived at the hotel in Boston was call Billy in his room.

"Oh, good," he said when he heard my voice. "I heard you were called up. Come on to my room."

I went up to his room and waited for him to get dressed so we could go down and go to breakfast.

"Do you mind if we have a couple of guests join us for breakfast?" he said. "I had already made the arrangements before you got here."

"Of course not," I said.

We go to the lobby and standing there waiting for us are two of the most beautiful blondes I have ever seen in my life. A couple of knockouts. Now, here we are, two rookies, one just up from the minor leagues that day, and we're parading through the lobby of the Kenmore Hotel with these gorgeous blondes. And the older guys like Allie Reynolds and Bobby Brown are standing there glaring at us because it looks like the girls have just come with us from our rooms. I hadn't even checked into my room, but it was a nice impression we made. By the way, I never saw those two girls again. I don't know about Billy. He's not talking.

We had an afternoon game that day and Tommy Byrne was our starting pitcher and of course the Red Sox always had strong right-handed hitting. Byrne is a left-hander and the Red Sox just ate him up. They banged him around for about eight runs in the first four innings and then Casey brought me in.

He probably felt the game was gone anyway so this would be a good day for me to get a few innings under my belt, to help get my feet on the ground.

I came in and took my warm-up pitches. The Sox had this fearsome lineup in those days: Ted Williams, Walt Dropo, Bobby Doerr, Vern Stephens, Dom DiMaggio, Johnny Pesky, Billy Goodman. What a lineup. The only weak spot they had was Birdie Tebbetts.

I was finished with my warm-ups and I started pitching. First pitch, single. Next pitch, another single. Next pitch, double. Then our first baseman, Tommy Henrich, came over to the mound.

"Hey, Eddie," he said, "that first-base coach knows everything you're throwing. He's calling every pitch."

I couldn't believe it because I had thrown only about six pitches. But it was true; Earle Combs, their first-base coach, was picking up my pitches. I was pitching from a stretch position and if I was going to throw a fastball, Combs would yell, "Be ready." If I was going to throw a curve, he'd tell the batter, "Make him get it up."

Henrich couldn't understand how he picked up my pitches so quickly and neither could I, until the next day when Jim Turner and Eddie Lopat took me on the sidelines and had me go through my sequence of pitches from the stretch position. They picked it up in almost no time.

What happened was that when I was going to throw a fastball from the stretch position, the inside of my wrist would lie flat against my stomach. But if I was going to throw a curveball, I would set the ball so that the side of my wrist was against my stomach. And is was easy for the first-base coach to spot this. Once I found out how I was tipping off my pitches, it was easy to correct it. But it was the kind of thing I had been doing for three years in the minor leagues without anybody ever picking it up.

I guarantee you, it never happened again. In fact, the next time I pitched against the Red Sox I could see Earle Combs staring at me from the first-base coach's box. But I never heard him shout to the hitters, "Be ready," or "Make him get it up."

About four days later, I started my first game against the Philadelphia Athletics in Yankee Stadium. I had to leave about sixty-five tickets for my friends, neighbors, and relatives. I left the game in the seventh inning with the score tied, 3–3, and wasn't involved in the decision.

I got my first win about five days after that, against the White Sox. I pitched seven innings and Tom Ferrick came in and pitched the eighth and ninth to save it for me. That whole season, from the time I got there until the last week, Casey pitched me only against second-division teams. He spotted me against teams he thought I could beat. There were only eight teams in the league then, but he would never pitch me against the first-division teams like Cleveland, Detroit, and Boston. Instead, I pitched against the Washington Senators, Philadelphia Athletics, Chicago White Sox, and St. Louis Browns. I wasn't complaining, because I won my first seven decisions pitching against second-division teams.

Martin already had a roommate when I arrived, so they roomed me with Yogi Berra, who was rooming alone. I could understand why. As a roommate, Yogi was a royal pain in the ass.

We were the original odd couple. Yogi used to like to go to bed early and wake up early. I liked to go to bed late and sleep late. As you can imagine, there were problems.

Yogi was a creature of habit. He got up every morning at six and made sure he made enough noise in the room to wake me up. He'd want to have a conversation while he got dressed, and I wanted to sleep. Then he'd finally leave and go downstairs to buy a newspaper and have breakfast. An hour or so later, he'd come back to the room, making more noise and waking me up again, of course, and he'd get back into bed and go to sleep.

If I would come home late, I'd go into the room and it would be dark. Yogi would be in bed and I figured he was asleep, so I wouldn't put on the light. I would stumble around in the dark getting undressed, banging my toes. I'd get all ready for bed, go to the bathroom, then I'd come back and crawl into bed. As soon as I got into bed, Yogi would turn on the light and want to start talking. The pain in the ass was awake all the time.

Once we were in Chicago and I was scheduled to pitch a day game. Yogi went through his routine, getting up at six, getting dressed, going down for the paper and breakfast. He wanted me to join him, but I told him no.

"Let me sleep," I said. "I'm tired. But wake me up when you leave for the ballpark and I'll get up and take a cab out there."

He forgot to wake me. All of a sudden, the phone rang. It was Red Patterson, our public relations director.

"What the hell are you doing?" Red started yelling into my ear. "Don't you know you're pitching today? Casey is really pissed."

I asked Red what time it was.

"It's noon," he said. "The game is at one."

I jumped out of bed and got dressed as fast as I could. There wasn't even time for breakfast. Then I took a cab from the Del Prado Hotel to Comiskey Park. I arrived at the park at 12:30 and I was pitching at 1:00.

I ran into the dressing room and started putting on my uniform. I finally got out on the field at 12:45 and began to warm up. My teeth were almost chattering I was so scared.

To make me feel worse, a couple of old pros like Hank Bauer, Gene Woodling, and Allie Reynolds came over to me and said, "Hey, rookie, don't go fooling around with our money."

They did things like that in those days. Reynolds, in particular. Allie is an American Indian and everybody called him "Chief." He was the boss. Everybody looked up to Allie. We were all kind of afraid of him. I know I was and Mickey was and I think Billy was. Allie was a fierce competitor. He hated to lose and if you messed up, he'd look at you like he wanted to kill you. It got to the point that you wanted to do well if only to keep peace with Allie.

I had been with the club only about a month when I overslept in Chicago and I was scared shitless. Fortunately, I won the game, 2–0, and everything was all right.

When I asked Yogi why he didn't wake me, he gave me one of his typical, profound, philosophical answers.

"I forgot," he said.

By September, Stengel must have thought I was ready to step up to better competition because we went to Detroit for a big three-game series and I was penciled in to pitch one of the games. We started the series with a one-game lead. We lost the first game of the series, but won the second, and Casey started me in the third. I was matched against the veteran right-hander Dizzy Trout.

After eight innings, we were tied, 1–1. Joe DiMaggio hit a home run for us in the sixth or seventh and they scored on back-to-back doubles. I was the first hitter due up in the top of the ninth and I was sure Casey was going to take me out for a pinch hitter. But he surprised me and let me hit. I led off the inning with a walk and we wound up scoring seven runs that inning and won the game, 8–1. It was a big game for me and for the team. I was over the hump because it was the first time Casey let me pitch against a first-division team, and I won. And the victory put us in first place and we never left there.

We wound up winning the pennant by three games over the Detroit Tigers. I started twelve games, finished seven of them, and had a record of 9-1. I felt great. Now I was certain I could pitch in the major leagues and win.

First we had to deal with the Philadelphia Phillies, known as the "Whiz Kids." They had won the National League championship by beating the Dodgers on the final day of the season.

We swept the Phillies in four games, but it wasn't as easy as that sounds. Every game was close and could have gone either way.

The Series opened in Philadelphia and we had Vic Raschi, a twenty-one-game winner, ready for the opener. Vic was every bit as much the competitor as Reynolds, but he was quiet. He rarely had much to say. He would just glare at you like Reynolds, but Allie was the meaner of the two. Raschi was well liked, but he could be mean when he wanted to be, especially on the mound.

The Phillies had needed their starters to fight off the challenge from the Dodgers, so their manager, Eddie Sawyer, took a big gamble and named Jim Konstanty to start the first game. Konstanty hadn't started a game all year. He appeared in seventy-four games in the regular season, all in relief, and finished with a 16-7 record. He was so dominant, he was named the league's Most Valuable Player.

The gamble almost paid off. Konstanty was superb, allow-ing only one run and four hits in eight innings. But Raschi was better. He gave up two singles in the fifth and nothing else, winning the game, 1–0, on a two-hitter.

Game Two was another pitchers' duel and another nail-biter. Allie Reynolds hooked up with Robin Roberts in a sensational pitching battle. After nine innings, it was tied, 1–1, then Joe DiMaggio homered leading off the top of the tenth and we won, 2–1.

After that second game, we went to the train station for the ride back to New York. I happened to notice Dizzy Dean sitting in the station. Diz, who had been such a great pitcher with the St. Louis Cardinals, was working for the Yankees as a television announcer. So I walked up to him and I guess I was a little cocky by then and I said to Dizzy, "Now I know how you won thirty games in this bush league."

Dizzy got pissed, but he didn't stay mad long. He really was a terrific guy.

Game Three of the 1950 World Series was played in Yankee Stadium and again it was another brilliant pitchers' duel. Eddie Lopat started for us against Ken Heintzelman, a battle of crafty veteran left-handers.

We scored a run in the third and they tied it with a run in the sixth, and went ahead with a run in the seventh. We tied it in the bottom of the eighth on three walks and an error. Then we scored the winning run in the bottom of the ninth on singles by Gene Woodling, Phil Rizzuto, and Jerry Coleman after two were out. Tom Ferrick, who relieved Lopat in the ninth, was the winner and we were ahead in the Series, three games to none.

Stengel had named me to pitch the fourth game and now I had a chance to make it the clincher. I held them scoreless through the first eight innings and we scored two in the first and three in the sixth and took a 5–0 lead into the ninth. I needed only three more outs.

But the Phillies still had some fight left in them. "Puddin' Head" Jones led off with a single and I hit Del Ennis with a pitch. I got the next two hitters and I thought the game, and the Series, was over when Andy Seminick hit a drive to deep left. But Woodling had trouble with the sun and dropped it for an error to score two runs and cut our lead to 5–2.

I thought I had a shutout, but I couldn't blame Woodling. Left field is tough to play, especially in October. A lot of out-fielders have had trouble with the sun out there at that time of year.

I wanted to finish, but when Mike Goliat singled, the Phillies brought the tying run to the plate. And that brought Casey to the mound to make a pitching change. He took me out, and it was the worst booing I ever heard Casey take at the Stadium. Half of the people booing were my family and friends. They booed the shit out of him. But he was right. I was getting tired and they had Stan Lopata, a right-handed power hitter, ready to come up as a pinch hitter.

Casey brought in Allie Reynolds. The old man wasn't fooling around. He wanted to end it here and now. It was getting dark and the shadows were falling in Yankee Stadium. Usually, the first place the shadow falls is around home plate, which makes it even harder to pick up the ball because it's coming out of light into dark. Lopata had no chance. Reynolds just pumped three fastballs past him and that was that. Lopata swung, but I'm not sure he ever even saw the ball.

It had been a great year, but a hectic one. I was looking forward to doing nothing all winter except collect my World Series check, maybe buy some clothes, and just hang around and wait to report to spring training again.

About two weeks after the Series, I was having a couple of beers with my friend Joe Gallagher in an Astoria bar called The Two-Way Inn. We were just up the street from the Con Ed building, which is also where the draft board was. I was eligible for the draft, and I was curious to know when I could expect my call-up. I was wondering how much of the 1951 season I might have to miss.

"Let's go to the draft board," I told Joe. "I want to find out when I can expect to be called."

We walked up to the draft board and I asked the lady behind the desk if she could tell me when I could expect my call. She asked my name and address and I told her and she went away to look something up. A few minutes later, she came back and said, "You're leaving in two weeks."

To say I was shocked would be a gross understatement. One day I was sitting on top of the world, a member of the world champion New York Yankees, the winner of the game that clinched the world championship, and the next day I faced the prospect of army life, basic training, peeling potatoes, long marches, and all the rest.

In times like these, when I was down about something, depressed or disappointed, I found there was only one thing to do. Have a party. To be honest, that wasn't a much different approach than I took when I was up, feeling good about something.

This time the party was my mom's idea. My reporting date was November 19, 1950, a Monday. About a week before I was scheduled to leave, Mom said, "Let's have a party." Good old mom, she always knew how to lift my spirits.

The party started at eight o'clock on a Friday night in our little two-bedroom apartment in Astoria. I invited some of the guys I had played ball with in the minor leagues who lived in the area, like Frank Verdi and Tommy Gorman. My father invited some of his bartender friends. The bartenders who worked late came after the bars had closed at about 2 A.M. that first night and, naturally, they weren't ready to leave right away, so before you knew it, the party had run into Saturday. Then those bartenders would have to leave and the ones who had the early shift would be getting off work and they would show up. It got to be a joke every time a new group of bartenders arrived. And this went on for three days, people coming and going, bartenders arriving after their shift and leaving when it was time to go to work. And every time they arrived, they'd bring another case of bottles with them from the bar.

The next thing I knew, it was almost Monday morning and I was scheduled to be at the induction center on Whitehall Street in lower Manhattan. I hadn't slept a wink in almost three days.

By Monday morning, you can bet that two-bedroom apartment was a mess from all the people who had trampled through it. There were people sleeping in chairs in the kitchen and the kitchen table was covered with liquor bottles. All of a sudden, there was a knock on the door and in walked a photographer from one of the New York papers. He had come, unannounced, to get a picture of me going off to the army.

He said he was hoping to get a picture of my mother making me my farewell breakfast. Little did he know he would be walking into a three-day party and find the kitchen table covered with booze bottles.

My mother had a hangover. I was still half buzzed. But this photographer had come all the way to Astoria for his picture and we didn't want to disappoint him. My mother and Joan started clearing all the bottles off the table and my mother took out a box of Wheaties and a bottle of milk and set them down on the table. And the photographer took his picture. I was supposed to be eating breakfast. My farewell breakfast, Wheaties and milk. The thought of it almost made me throw up.

It wasn't long after I went into the army that I met Mickey Mantle for the first time. I remember it well. It was on my wedding day.

By this time, as you may recall, I had been going steady with Joan Foran, the girl from across the street, for years. We had just sort of agreed that we would get married when I had saved some money. The combination of my first year with the Yankees and my first World Series check, plus the fact that I had been drafted and we faced the prospect of being apart for two years, made us decide to get married right away.

Our wedding date was April 14, 1951. We got married in St. Patrick's Church in Long Island City. The reception was in Donahue's bar in Astoria, a nice place on Steinway Street with an upstairs room that seated about 150 people.

Just as a courtesy, Joan's mother sent a wedding invitation to Red Patterson, publicity director of the Yankees. We never expected anybody from the team to show. It was actually meant more as an announcement than an invitation.

In those days, the Yankees and Dodgers would always play three games in New York, either at Yankee Stadium or at Ebbets Field, on the weekend just before the start of the regular season. As it turned out, that year it happened to be the weekend of our wedding.

Wouldn't you know it? After the wedding ceremony, our one limousine pulls up at Donahue's and just as we do, a bus pulls up and there's the whole Yankees team. It took us completely by surprise. We had no idea they were coming. Nobody ever told us. I think Casey Stengel made them come and, of course, I was very pleased and the neighborhood flipped. The team had just come back from spring training in Phoenix and they had played against the Dodgers in Ebbets Field that afternoon, then they all got on the bus and came to Astoria. I'm sure the last thing those guys wanted to do was go to a wedding, but they were there and you can imagine the excitement it created. Joe DiMaggio on Steinway Street! It was great. My neighbors couldn't believe it. I don't think the neighborhood has gotten over it yet.

In those days, at a wedding reception, especially in a place like Donahue's, it was customary to set up a Manhattan cocktail in front of each place setting, and I remember Joe Di-Maggio and Joe Page and Tommy Henrich and some of the other veteran players going around the room stopping at each table and knocking down the Manhattans. They must have had about four or five each.

I thought it was nice that the team came. We all did. They didn't stay more than about thirty or forty minutes, but it was great.

I remember meeting Mickey Mantle on the bus. He was too shy to get off and come in to the reception, so Joan and I went onto the bus to shake hands with the few players who'd stayed on. And Mick was one of them.

I had seen Mantle before, but never met him. He was still in the minor leagues when I came up in the second half of the 1950 season. The one time I saw him was late in the 1950 season when he and a left-handed pitcher named Bob Wiesler came up to work out with the team. They had just finished their season at Joplin, Mo., and the Yankees had them join us on a western trip so the club could take a look at these prospects and they could get a taste of major league life. Later in the trip, we were joined by another Yankee prospect, a kid named Bill "Moose" Skowron they had signed out of Purdue University, where he had been a punter on the football team.

I remember Mantle joining us in St. Louis, and that was the first time I ever saw him. I didn't meet him. He was so shy, he didn't talk to anybody but Wiesler for the two weeks he was with us. But I remember him and Moose taking batting practice with us before the games and they put on a great show of power hitting. They were both very impressive for kids so young.

Now he was at my wedding reception. Rather, he was in a bus parked outside where my wedding reception was being held. He had been with the Yankees in spring training and made the team. Joan and I went out to the bus and I formally met Mantle for the first time.

I remember my impression of him the first time I met him. I thought, "What a hayseed."

Years later, Mick told me what he was thinking when we first met.

"I was thinking I'd sure like to get to know Joanie a little better," he said.

CHAPTER 3

Army life was rough. Would you believe it, they actually wanted me to pitch three times a week. I refused and that almost caused me to get court-martialed. But I'm getting slightly ahead of myself.

I had been in the army five months when I took a thirteen-day furlough so Joan and I could get married. We had planned to leave right after the wedding to honeymoon in Florida, but the Yankees asked me if I could delay my plans a few days and throw out the first ball on Opening Day, wearing my army uniform.

I was flattered and Joan agreed, so I accepted. The wedding was on a Saturday. The opener was the following Tuesday, so it meant delaying our honeymoon trip just three days. We spent the three days at the Park Sheraton Hotel.

I threw out the first ball of the 1951 season and we were to leave for Florida that night. Joan and I watched the game from the box right next to the Yankees dugout. In order to get out faster and avoid the crowd, when the game was over we were to go through the dugout and out the nearest exit.

When the game was over we headed for the dugout. But the steps leading down to the dugout are very steep and Joan tripped on her high heels and fell down the steps. She tore her stockings and cut her knee, which is a nice way to start your honeymoon.

A friend of mine named Frankie Dolan was running the Park Sheraton Hotel in those days and he had asked us where we were going on our honeymoon. We told him we were going to Florida, but we had no specific plans, so he gave us a letter and told us to go to the Ambassador Hotel in Palm Beach and everything would be set up for us.

We went down to Palm Beach, went to the Ambassador Hotel, and looked up the man Frankie told us to see. Everything had been arranged. He put us in this beautiful, luxurious one-bedroom suite. Every day, there were fresh flowers in the room. There was also a refrigerator and they had it well stocked with beer and champagne. We were supposed to stay ten days, but after about a week, I was getting a little nervous, wondering how I was going to pay for all of that on my army salary. I had only a couple of hundred dollars with me.

"We'd better get home," I told Joan, who was just as nervous about the bill as I was.

We went to check out and I got the bill and the only thing on the bill was $11 for phone calls we had made to our folks back home. Frankie Dolan had arranged for everything.

While we were in Florida, I got a call from Bruce Henry. Bruce had been in the Yankees' organization for years. He would eventually wind up as our traveling secretary, but I first met him when I was playing for Norfolk in 1948 and he was the general manager. Now he was the general manager of the West Palm Beach Indians and he found out I was in the area and called to ask me if I would pitch batting practice one day.

"But, Bruce," I protested, "I'm on my honeymoon."

"Come on, coach," he said. Bruce called everybody "coach," women included. "It's only one day."

Bruce Henry had the ability to sell ice cubes to Eskimos and he talked me into pitching batting practice. What he didn't tell me was that he had already announced it all over Palm Beach and the place was sold out. He said it was the biggest crowd that ever came to see batting practice. In fact, it was his biggest crowd of the season.

I must say, though, that it didn't exactly thrill Joan to have her husband go off and pitch batting practice during her honeymoon. She got over it, and a lot of other unscheduled absences of mine, and we recently celebrated our thirty-sixth anniversary.

I should pause here to let you know about the rest of the Ford family. Joan and I have three children, each born a year apart, in 1952, 1953, and 1954.

Our oldest, Sally Ann, is married to Steve Clancy, and they have three children. My granddaughter Brett is eleven. My grandsons Evan and Craig are nine and five and they look like they may be pretty good athletes.

As a girl, Sally Ann competed a little in track and swimming, but nothing special. She was always very much the lady even when she was a little girl.

Our son Eddie came next. He played baseball at the University of South Carolina for Bobby Richardson, where he was a teammate of Ed Lynch, the pitcher for the New York Mets and Chicago Cubs. Eddie signed with the Boston Red Sox and got as far as triple A. I always thought he was a prospect. He was a major league fielder. Unfortunately, he never hit enough, about .220 or .230, which would be good enough now for a shortstop, but wasn't when he was playing.

His biggest claim to fame was getting a hit off Ron Guidry that helped win a ball game in spring training.

George Steinbrenner almost had a heart attack that night. The game was on television back in New York and George always wanted to win the TV games in spring training, especially if they were against the Mets or our archrivals, the Red Sox.

The score was tied, 2–2, in the ninth and Eddie led off with a single against Guidry. He stole second and, with two out, Carl Yastrzemski singled and Eddie scored the winning run. George went berserk. We had lost to the hated Red Sox in a televised game, and that was unforgivable.

"How the hell can you have this guy Guidry pitching in the late innings with the game on the line?" he wanted to know.

This was Guidry's first year and George was ready to ship him and the pitching coach, Cloyd Boyer, out on the spot.

I was coaching first base and I figured I was in trouble with George because my Eddie had gotten the hit that led to the winning run. But actually, George was very gracious. He eventually calmed down and later told me, "Your boy looked pretty good tonight."

But he was so mad at Guidry and Boyer. George has gotten a lot better, but in those days he would want to get rid of that pitcher and that pitching coach right on the spot. Of course, Guidry went on to be 16-7 that year.

Eddie played about three or four seasons in the minor leagues, then he realized he wasn't going to make it to the majors, so he packed it in and got involved on Wall Street.

Our youngest, Tommy, was every bit as good an athlete as Eddie, he just didn't apply himself to baseball as much as Eddie did. Tommy was more interested in swimming and diving. I'm convinced that if Tommy had put more into baseball, he could have had a career in the game. He was a left-handed pitcher. His biggest thrill in baseball was when he struck his brother out in a game once. They went to different high schools. Eddie went to Great Neck South because he wanted to play football. Tommy went to St. Mary's in Manhasset, which didn't have a football team. One day, Great Neck South played St. Mary's in baseball and Tommy struck Eddie out with a big, slow curve-ball. Eddie heard about it for the rest of the week.

Today, Tommy is a black belt in karate. He works on Wall Street with Fundamental Brokers, a company I do some work for. They deal in government bonds.

Let me correct a common misconception about being a father and a baseball player traveling around the country so much. For one thing, the traveling in my day wasn't that bad. We'd be away about eighty days a year. But look at all the time I spent with my family. I have often maintained that when I was playing ball and my children were growing up, I spent more time with my family than most fathers do.

The average guy who works nine to five, five days a week, usually leaves for work before his kids are awake. He comes home six or seven at night, has dinner, the kids do their homework, and then they go to sleep. Weekends, he's playing golf or watching television.

I had my kids in spring training, two or three months every year. I'd spend a few hours at the ballpark and the rest of the time I was with them. When we played night games, I'd have all day at home with them before they were of school age or when school was out. The season would end in early October and I'd be home most of October, all of November, December, January, and February, until we all went to spring training.

I can't believe the average working man has that much time with his family. I would even take my family on road trips occasionally. They'd come on the short trips to Boston, Baltimore, and Washington. Once I even took them to California, so they could go to Disneyland.

The only bad time was when the kids were little and I had to leave for two weeks. We had three children in three years and I would have to leave Joan with three kids in diapers. Fortunately, she had her sisters, Sally and Margaret, and her mother and my mother to help out.

The one thing I did miss was seeing my boys play Little League. Their games would be on Saturday afternoon or Tuesday and Thursday nights, and I was either traveling or playing ball myself. I missed that.

But when Tommy and Eddie were twelve and thirteen, I started taking them to Yankee Stadium. They'd come out on the field before the game and I'd pitch batting practice to them. I remember Frank Crosetti taking Eddie aside and giving him tips on how to play shortstop. That helped him a lot.

Getting back to my army career, I was stationed at Fort Monmouth, N.J., and my job was to pitch for their baseball team, which wasn't bad duty. But the commanding officer had the idea that I should pitch three times a week.

The manager of the team was a civilian named Mule Haas, who had played twelve years in the major leagues with the Pirates, the White Sox, and the Athletics. It wasn't his idea that I pitch three times a week, but he was under orders.

"Mule," I argued, "I'm twenty-two years old. I want to be able to pitch for the Yankees when I get out of here."

"I agree with you, Whitey," Mule said. "But I mentioned it to the general and he said, 'No, I want him to pitch three times a week.' He said it's good for morale and we get bigger crowds when you pitch."

So I quit the team and joined the Monmouth Beach Inn softball team and played with them the rest of my army hitch to stay in shape. I never did get court-martialed. I mean, it wasn't like I was a traitor or something.

While I was in the army, I supplemented my meager salary by playing baseball and basketball on weekends when I was able to get a three-day pass. This was all through the efforts of a man named Pete Petropoulous, who is a story in himself.

I have known Pete since I was fourteen. He had been a pitcher in the Giants' organization, a five-foot-six, 145-pound left-hander. He pitched in the Florida State League until World War II interrupted his career.

He had been wounded in the war and they said he would never walk again. But they didn't know about Pete's spirit and courage. He started out in a wheelchair, then went to crutches, then to a cane. Today, Pete lives in Georgia with his wife, Gloria, and he walks without a limp. To see him scoot around, you'd never know he ever had a problem.

After the war, Pete started hanging around the Polo Grounds with the Giants, and then Chesterfield, the cigarette company, hired him to be a kind of goodwill ambassador. Every time a Giants player hit a home run, Chesterfield, which sponsored their games on radio and television, would donate cartons of cigarettes to veterans' hospitals in the area. It was Pete's job to deliver the cigarettes.

Pete also had this basketball team, the Chesterfield Satisfiers, and they would go around playing games for charity, or to entertain the wounded veterans. Then he got the idea that he could make a little money doing the same thing, so he put together the Whitey Ford All-Stars, and we would play games in upstate New York towns like Poughkeepsie, Peekskill, and Binghamton. We'd play baseball in the summer and basketball in the winter.

In basketball, Pete also supplied the opposition. He had the Detroit Clowns, the St. Louis Bombers, and the Masked Marvels.

In the winter of 1950–51, he scheduled a basketball game in Binghamton for the Whitey Ford All-Stars because I had just won that World Series game for the Yankees, but especially because I had won sixteen games for Binghamton in 1949, helped them win a championship, and was something of a local hero.

When Pete booked the game in Binghamton, the local promoter wanted to know who our opponents would be.

"I have the St. Louis Bombers," Pete said.

"We had them last year," the promoter said. "Can't you get another team?"

"Yeah," said Pete, "I'll get the Masked Marvels."

It was easy for Pete to deliver the Masked Marvels. All he had to do was go up to his attic, where he kept all these uniforms—the Detroit Clowns, the St. Louis Bombers, the Masked Marvels. He used the same guys, a bunch of really good semipro players from Harlem. He just changed their uniforms.

That satisfied the people in Binghamton and they promoted the Whitey Ford All-Stars vs. the Masked Marvels at the Endicott-Johnson Arena and they sold out the place. More than four thousand people showed up, presumably some of them because they were curious to see Whitey Ford play basketball.

We had some good players: Connie Simmons and Dick Surhoff, who had played with the Knicks, and Connie's brother, Johnny, my minor league teammate who had spent some time with the Boston Celtics. I wasn't a very good basketball player and I didn't want to take any chances of breaking my ankle, but it was my team and I had to play. At least I had to try.

"All right, Whitey," Pete said. "You're going to start the game and we're going to keep feeding the ball to you and you keep shooting. As soon as you score a basket, fall on the floor and grab your ankle and we'll carry you off the court and you'll be through for the night."

Surhoff and the Simmons brothers kept getting rebounds and they kept passing the ball to me, but I was missing layup after layup. I was horrible. I just couldn't hit a shot. I missed so many shots that we were behind something like 18–2.

Then I finally made one and I did what Pete instructed me to do. I fell down on the floor, grabbing my ankle. And the rest of the guys went into their act. They put some ice on the ankle and they carried me off the court.

Pete had an announcement made to the crowd: "Whitey Ford has a possible fractured ankle. He will not be able to return to the game."

Nobody seemed to mind. They had seen enough of me, anyway. And without me to drag them down, the Whitey Ford All-Stars caught up to the Masked Marvels and won the game.

That was the end of my budding basketball career.

I was discharged from the army in November 1952, and guess what was the first thing I did? That's right, I had a party. There were about twenty of us from the New York area who went into the army together and spent the two years at Fort Monmouth together, so when we got out we decided to have a "getting out of the army" party.

One of the guys arranged for us to meet at this rathskeller in New York City, but when we got there, we discovered that the place didn't have a private room. We would have to have our party in the main dining room, with all the other diners, and that wasn't exactly what we had in mind.

I suddenly got an idea. I had met Toots Shor during the 1950 World Series. I was standing in the lobby of the Warwick Hotel and Toots was there with his wife, Baby. He recognized me and he came up and introduced himself. Toots was a big baseball fan and he was the owner of the most famous sports bar in the world on Fifty-first Street in Manhattan.

I started going to Toots's place that winter and I got to be pretty good friends with him. In later years, he would come to be one of my best friends.

This is the kind of man Toots Shor was. One night I was in his place and we were talking and I happened to mention that I was looking for a television set. The next day, he had a TV set delivered to my house. That was Toots. He was a very generous man, almost to a fault.

So when we discovered the problem at that rathskeller, I called Toots and told him my situation: I was with about twenty guys who had just been discharged from the army and we were looking for a place with a private room to have a party. He told us to come right over, and he gave us an upstairs room in his place all for ourselves, and we had a great time.

From then on, I started spending a lot of time in Toots's and we got to be very close.

My brother-in-law, Bobby Bartels, who is married to Joan's youngest sister, Margaret Ann, was boxing professionally. One night, he fought a main event in Madison Square Garden against Lenny Mangiapane. It was one of those neighborhood ethnic fights that usually did good business at the Garden.

There were about four thousand Italians from Corona rooting for Mangiapane and about four thousand Irishmen from the longshoremen's union rooting for Bobby, and a big riot broke out in the arena. Bobby knocked Lenny down and Lenny wasn't really hurt, but he climbed out of the ring.

Somebody threw a bottle into the ring and it hit Bobby's manager, Big Julie Isaacson, on the head. Toots was there with Baby and Yogi Berra and his wife, Carmen. As soon as I saw Big Julie get hit with the bottle, I told Toots and Yogi, "You better get your wives out of here because there's going to be a riot."

I hustled Margaret Ann into Bobby's dressing room and the last thing I saw was Yogi and Toots running up the aisle, with Baby and Carmen about twenty feet behind them.

Just about everybody who was anybody in sports and entertainment used to drop in at Toots's when he and Baby were in town. Through Toots, I got to meet people like Cardinal Spellman, Frank Sinatra, Don Ameche, Ty Cobb, Horace McMahon, Frankie Frisch, Lou Costello, and The Great One himself, Jackie Gleason.

Whenever Gleason was in town, he'd hang out at Toots's and what times they used to have. I never laughed so hard as I did when Toots and Gleason got together.

Toots and Jackie were the best of friends, but they were also very competitive. They always used to argue about who could drink the most and, believe me, they both could drink.

One afternoon they decided to have a drinking contest to decide, once and for all, who could drink the most. It was 1:30, the lunch crowd had left, and the place was practically empty. Toots challenged Gleason to a drinking contest and Gleason accepted, so they got a bottle of brandy for Toots and a bottle of Scotch for Gleason and they started drinking.

All of a sudden, Gleason got up to go to the bathroom and he passed out right on the floor. The waiters came over and started to pick him up but Toots wouldn't let them.

"Let him lay there," he said.

Another time, they decided to have a race around the block. They went out in front of the place on Fifty-first Street and Toots was supposed to run toward Fifth Avenue and around and Gleason was supposed to run toward Sixth Avenue and around, and the first one back at the place was to be the winner.

So, Toots headed for Fifth Avenue and he ran around the block, and he came back to the place puffing like hell, and there was Gleason sitting at the bar having a drink.

"Where have you been, pal of mine?" Gleason said to Toots.

"How the hell did you get back here so quick?" Toots said.

And Gleason just smiled that cocky smile of his. About fifteen minutes passed and it suddenly occurred to Toots that something was wrong.

"Hey," he said, "how come I never passed you on the street?"

What happened was Gleason went outside, started running toward Sixth Avenue while Toots was running in the opposite direction, then as soon as he turned the corner, Jackie hailed a taxi and had it take him back to Toots's place.

Gleason could never resist a challenge. One time we were in there drinking with him, Billy Martin and I, and Gleason and Martin got to talking about bowling. The next thing you know, Gleason is challenging Billy to a bowling match. As it turned out Billy is a pretty good bowler and he beat Gleason for a couple of hundred dollars. With the money, Billy went out and bought a pair of alligator cowboy boots. After that, every time Billy saw Gleason, if he had the cowboy boots on, he couldn't resist showing them to Gleason and thanking him for buying him the boots.

One time—this was in the early sixties—Gleason invited me to spend ten days with him at the Doral Hotel on Miami Beach. He was doing his shows from down there, but he would work only two days a week, so that meant we had the rest of the time to hang out.

The reason he had me down there was he had set up the "World Championship of Golf," just the two of us, the best out of seven. He had these two trophies made up, a great big one for the winner and a tiny one for the loser, and he had the trophies inscribed THE GLEASON-FORD GOLF CHAMPION-SHIP. I beat him, four out of seven.

One day it rained and we couldn't play golf so he invited me to play pool instead. Everybody knows Gleason is a very good pool player, but I accepted because he said he would spot me a lead. He spotted me 50–35 and I beat him. Then he spotted me 50–45, and I beat him again. Now he was really getting pissed off and he said, "One more game, double or nothing."

I was ahead $1,200, so I said, "Nothing doing. I'm playing for two hours and I'm ahead twelve hundred dollars and you want me to blow it all back in a few minutes. I'll tell you what. I'll play you one game even for six hundred dollars."

And he looked at me and in that way of his he said, "YOU'LL play ME even!"

We played and he beat me, but it was close, about 50–42, because as good a player as he is, Gleason doesn't play very well when he's had a couple of bottles of champagne. I couldn't wait to call Toots and tell him I beat Gleason for $600 playing pool. And until the day Toots died, he never let Gleason live it down.

There were many reasons why I was happy to be out of the army and looking forward to rejoining the Yankees for the 1953 season, not the least of which was that I was broke and I expected to get a good contract because of the contribution I had made to the 1950 world championship.

Joan and I were living in a tiny apartment in Jackson Heights, Queens, and we already had Sally Ann. A block away from our apartment was the Miami bar. That winter, to give Joan a break, I would take Sally Ann for a walk in her carriage and I'd usually end up going into the Miami bar for a beer. I'd put Sally Ann's carriage near the jukebox and put a dime in and let her listen to the music while I would go up to the bar for my beer.

And just about every day, there was this young guy sitting at the bar, a guy about my age. We started up a friendship, but I never did get to know the guy's name, who he was, what he did, or why he was in the bar almost every day. I'd buy him a beer and he'd buy me back and we'd talk for a few minutes and I would leave. This must have happened at least fifteen or twenty afternoons that winter.

After that I never saw the guy again until many years later, when I went to Texas to play in an Old-timers Game. Billy Martin was managing the Rangers at the time and another old teammate Bobby Brown, was the vice-president of the club.

We were at the ballpark and Bobby brought this guy over to me and said, "Whitey, I'd like you to meet the owner of the Texas Rangers, Brad Corbett."

"Hello, Brad," I said, extending my hand.

"You don't remember me, do you?" he said.

"Should I?"

"Do you remember the Miami bar in Jackson Heights? You used to bring your daughter in almost every day in her carriage and put her near the jukebox and you'd have a beer with some guy at the bar."

"Was that you?"

"Yep."

"What are you doing owning the Texas Rangers?"

Corbett went on to explain that he had invented a new underground plastic pipe for sprinkler systems, started a company called Robin Tech, made a lot of money, and bought the ball club.

"It happened right after I met you in the Miami bar," Corbett said.

"I wondered whatever happened to you," I said.

Here it was twenty years later and I meet this guy at an Old-timers Game in Texas. Talk about it being a small world.

As a rookie in 1950, I had been paid at the annual rate of $5,000 for the little more than two months I was with the team. I figured I should be worth at least $10,000 for 1953. Needless to say, I was disappointed, shocked, and pissed off when I received my contract and it called for $6,000, a $1,000 raise.

I went to see George Weiss, the Yankees' general manager, and his assistant, Roy Hamey, and told them I wanted $10,000. They almost fainted. I must admit they had a pretty good argument against me. The team had won the world championship without me in 1951 and 1952 and they felt they could win it again without me. They didn't make me feel wanted.

But I thought I also had a good argument.

"I won nine games for you in 1950," I said. "And I lost only one and we won the pennant by two games. I think I might have had something to do with us winning the pennant."

They both started screaming at me.

"You've been in the army," they said. "You haven't pitched in two years. How do we know you can still pitch?"

I didn't know what to say. I didn't know how to negotiate in those days. And there weren't any agents around then. If I had walked in there with an agent or a lawyer, Weiss would have thrown us out on our ears. They really had me, and all players, over the barrel back then. They could give us whatever they wanted to and we had no choice.

Finally, they softened and said they'd give me $8,000.

"Nope," I said. "I won't sign for anything less than nine thousand dollars."

"If you're not on the next plane to St. Petersburg," Weiss said, "I'm going to cut our offer to seven thousand."

You have to picture this. Joan and I are living in this little apartment in Jackson Heights. Sally Ann is a year old and Joan is expecting another baby. And I have no money in the bank and no skills to do anything but play baseball. I signed for the $8,000 and headed for spring training.

When I reported there, Pete Sheehy, our equipment manager, gave me a different uniform number. I had worn number 19 in 1950, but that was taken by Ray Scarborough and it really didn't have any special meaning for me, so it didn't really matter when Pete assigned me number 16 in 1953. That number had been worn by a pitcher named Ernie Nevel in 1950, but he was no longer with the club.

I never was very big on numbers and their significance, mainly because I am not a superstitious person. What concerned me more than the number I wore was the fact that I had a terrible spring training in 1953, probably because of the two-year army layoff. I thought I'd improve after some time passed, but I was worried about what Casey and Jim Turner were thinking.

The big three of Vic Raschi, Allie Reynolds, and Eddie Lopat was still there and the veteran Johnny Sain had come over from the Boston Braves in 1951 and was in the starting rotation. I was not in the rotation when the season opened.

I didn't get my first start until about ten days into the season, but I wound up having a good year, 18-6, with eleven complete games, and led our staff in wins.

We wound up winning ninety-nine games that season and beat the Cleveland Indians by eight and a half games, then faced the Brooklyn Dodgers in the World Series.

It was the Yankees' fifth consecutive pennant, but only my second, and I was happy because it meant I would be getting a World Series check. Heaven knows, I really needed the money.

Reynolds started the first game of the 1953 World Series against Carl Erskine in Yankee Stadium. We beat them, 9–5, with Billy Martin hitting a triple and two singles and driving in three runs. Erskine lasted one inning and Sain won the game in relief of Reynolds.

Lopat beat Preacher Roe in the second game and the Dodgers brought Erskine back to pitch the third game against Raschi in Brooklyn. Erskine had this big breaking curveball and he really had it going for him that day. He struck out fourteen of us, including Mickey Mantle and Joe Collins four times each.

I remember sitting next to Johnny Mize during the game. John was a big hulking Southerner who had once hit fifty-one home runs in a season for the Giants. He was past his prime by then and he could hardly move, but he still had a terrific batting eye. We got him to be a pinch hitter and he won many games for us with his bat.

Mize had played most of his career in the National League and had batted against Erskine many times. So in this game he was sitting in the dugout, chewing tobacco and spraying tobacco juice all over the dugout floor and he was watching Erskine ring up these strikeouts with his curveball. And every time Erskine struck out another hitter, Mize would spit a spray of tobacco juice and say, "How the hell can those guys keep swinging at those curveballs in the dirt? You got to lay off that pitch. They're balls. Make him come in with the ball."

This went on for eight innings. Then in the top of the ninth, with the Dodgers leading, 3–2, and one out, Casey sent Mize up to pinch-hit. And John struck out on a curveball in the dirt. It was Erskine's fourteenth strikeout, setting a World Series record. I couldn't help laughing to myself.

I started the fourth game in Ebbets Field against my old Astoria buddy Billy Loes, and I had nothing. The Dodgers scored three runs off me in the first inning and Casey took me out at the start of the second, and the Dodgers beat us to even the Series at two games apiece.

Nobody knew who was going to start for us in Game Five. I'm not sure Casey even knew until almost game time. He had decided he would keep Reynolds in the bullpen for the re-mainder of the Series, figuring if he got a lead, he could use Allie twice, maybe three more times, to save the game. That still left us without a starting pitcher for Game Five and there was a lot of speculation in the newspapers over who it would be.

We had a left-hander named Bill Miller, who had started only three games for us all season. Miller had about as much chance of pitching that fifth game as the man in the moon, especially since he was a left-hander and we were playing at Ebbets Field. But Miller didn't know that. And Bob Kuzava, who liked to play a practical joke now and again, knew that Miller didn't know that.

SLICK

Frank Crosetti, our third-base coach, was in charge of the baseballs and one of the things he liked to do was get a brand new baseball and stick it in the shoe of the pitcher who was going to start that day. Sometimes a pitcher wouldn't find out he was starting until he came to the ballpark and saw the brand new baseball in his shoe.

This gave Kuzava an idea. He was tuned in to all the little idiosyncrasies around the club and, like a good practical joker, he knew the personalities of his victims.

We went to Ebbets Field and into the clubhouse and the first thing Miller did was undress, then go into the bathroom to shave. While he was shaving, Kuzava took a new baseball and put it in his shoe. Then Kuzava went into the bathroom, went up to Miller, and said, "Good luck today, Bill."

"What do you mean?" Miller said.

"You're pitching today," Kuzava said.

"Me?" asked Miller, who by now was turning white, and I don't mean because of the shaving cream on his face.

"Look in your shoe."

Miller turned and looked in his shoe, and there was the baseball. He had come to the park not expecting even to pitch at all and now he believed he was the starting pitcher in the fifth game of the World Series against the Dodgers in Ebbets Field. He almost cut himself shaving.

The guy who did get the start was almost as much of a surprise as Miller. It was Jim McDonald, a right-hander who had won nine games for us during the regular season. Mac was knocked around for six runs, but we got home runs from Mickey Mantle, Billy Martin, Gil McDougald, and Gene Woodling. And McDonald kept us in the game until the eighth inning. Then Kuzava and Reynolds finished it off, and we won, 11–7, to take a 3-2 lead back to Yankee Stadium.

I was happy that Casey decided to bring me back for Game Six because I wanted to atone for pitching so badly in the fourth game.

Erskine was trying to come back on two days' rest and he just couldn't do it. He didn't have that sharp-breaking curveball and we scored two off him in the first inning and one more in the second. We should have scored two runs in the second, not one. It was my fault that we didn't.

I was on third base with one out and Yogi hit a drive that Duke Snider caught in deep center. I could have walked home, but I tagged up at third and left before Snider made the catch. Third-base coach Frank Crosetti yelled for me to come back and tag up again, which I did, but in the time I lost, they threw me out at home. I was so embarrassed doing such a dumb thing like that in front of all my friends and neighbors. Worse than that, it could have cost us the game. It did cost me a World Series victory.

Instead of the score being 4–1, it was 3–1 when Casey took me out and brought in Allie Reynolds to pitch the last two innings and nail down the Series. But Carl Furillo hit a two-run homer off Reynolds with one out in the ninth to tie it at 3–3, and that meant I could not be the winner.

We won the game, and the Series, in the bottom of the ninth, when Martin singled in the winning run against Clem Labine. It was his twelfth hit of the Series, and it tied a World Series record for most hits in a six-game Series.

I didn't get the win, but I was happy. The Yankees had won their fifth straight world championship. I had won two world championships in my two years in the major leagues. But most important, I collected a World Series check for $8,281. That meant Joan and I could finally move out of our apartment in Jackson Heights. We used the money for a down payment on our first house, in Glen Cove, although my check was for $1,000 less than it should have been.

What happened was that on the night we clinched the pennant, Mickey, Billy, and I went out to the Latin Quarter. The bill came to $80, and as a joke, I signed the name of the Yankees' co-owner Dan Topping to the check. I put our names down, then signed the check "Dan Topping." I figured Topping would get a laugh out of that and we'd just reimburse him the $80.

Instead, the next day we got a call from somebody in the Yankee office saying we were each fined $1,000.

The next week we won the World Series, and at the victory party Billy and Mickey went over to Topping at the bar, and he wrote them each a check for $1,000, returning the fine. Then they came over to me and said, "Go over there—Topping will write you a check for a thousand dollars."

"Tell him I said to stick it," I told them.

I was too proud to go begging, but the next spring he did return the fine.

I liked Topping and his partner, Del Webb. They were quite unlike George Steinbrenner, who is very involved in his team. Topping and Webb were owners who remained in the background. You would see them only after we won the final game of the World Series, when they would come into the clubhouse. Or you might see them at the victory party or occasionally if you were negotiating a contract.

Mostly they let George Weiss handle the contract talks. Weiss was a hard-liner, but if he couldn't resolve a contract dispute—especially with the big guys like Mickey and DiMag—then Topping and Webb would step in, and they usually gave in to the players.

*   *   *

We won 103 games in 1954 and I was 16-8 and even picked up a save in relief. But we didn't win the pennant. That was the year the Cleveland Indians won 111 games and beat us out.

To add insult to injury, that year I had one of my most embarrassing moments.

We were playing in Washington and President Eisenhower attended the game, and I really wanted to pitch a good game with him in attendance. I pitched well to everybody but Jim Lemon, a big, tall right-handed slugger who always hit me like he had stock in me. Lemon hit three home runs off me. Fortunately, they all came with the bases empty.

Then it was the ninth inning and we were leading, 5–3, and I had two out, and then somebody got a single and here came Lemon to the plate. And here came Stengel to the mound.

"Let me stay in, Case," I said. "I'll get him this time."

"What are you, out of your damn mind?" Stengel said. "The guy already hit three home runs. You want to try for four?"

So Casey waved to the bullpen and brought in Tom Morgan, who got Lemon out, and we won the game.

Joan just couldn't believe I wasn't going to get a World Series check in 1954. We had been counting on it because we had just moved to that house in the suburbs.

Fortunately, Frank Scott, the first of the player agents, came up with a deal that meant I could make $1,500. Some guy named Rhinelander had asked Scott to put together an all-star team to play three games in Hawaii, and Scott asked me to go along with Harvey Kuenn, Carl Erskine, Duke Snider, Red Schoendienst, Hank Sauer, Del Crandall, Sammy White, Billy Goodman, and Bob Grim.

Our son Tommy had been born about two months before. Sally Ann was two and Eddie was one, and when I told Joan

SLICK

I was going off to Hawaii with the Frank Scott all-star team, she was more than a little pissed off.

"I'm going," I said. "We need the money."

Don't forget, $1,500 was a lot of money in those days.

I went to Hawaii and we played the three games, and the deal was we would get our money after the third game. So we went into the dressing room after the third game and Frank Scott said, "We can't find Rhinelander."

He was married to a Japanese woman and the next day we found out that he had skipped out with all our money and gone to Japan.

That wasn't the worst part. The worst part was coming home and confronting Joan. Not only had I left her alone with three little kids for ten days, I had to tell her that I never got the $1,500 I was promised and that I had spent a couple of hundred dollars in bar tabs hanging around with Harvey Kuenn.

CHAPTER

4

I began spending time with Mickey Mantle in 1953, my first year back from the army. From what little I knew about him at that point, I could never imagine having enough in common with Mickey to socialize with him. I figured we were incompatible. No two people could have been more different: me from the streets of New York, a know-it-all city kid, him a hick from Oklahoma.

While I was in the army, though, Mickey began hanging out with Billy Martin, so it was just natural for the three of us to get together when I returned. Most of the time we spent together was on road trips. When the team was in New York, I would go home to my family every night. Well, almost every night.

When I did see Mickey again, in 1953, he had changed. He had been in the major leagues for two years and had begun to take on a little sophistication. He was dressing nicely (no more jeans and cowboy boots) and he knew his way around. I'm sure Billy had something to do with that.

And when I saw him play, I couldn't believe how good he was—how fast he ran, how much power he had. I had seen him that week or two in 1950, when he came up from the minor leagues and traveled with us, and I had heard and read a lot about his tremendous potential. But now that potential had become a reality.

Back in 1950, he was a shortstop and a bad one. He could hardly pick up a ball, and when he did, he couldn't throw it straight. By 1953, they had converted him to the outfield. He wasn't a great outfielder at first, but he became one. In those days, he would just outrun balls with his great speed and he had a powerful throwing arm.

I caught my first glimpse of his great batting power in Washington, when he hit that tremendous home run against Chuck Stobbs. The ball sailed clear out of the stadium and traveled almost six hundred feet. I think that was when I first became convinced that I was in the company of greatness.

Looking back, there's no question that Mickey was the greatest ballplayer I ever saw. I'm not making any comparisons between Mick and Joe DiMaggio because I can't. It wouldn't be fair. I played with DiMag just one season, 1950, and by then he was at the end of his career and was having physical problems. In fact, I saw Joe only a little more than half a season. When I joined the club in July, he was batting about .235 and he ended up hitting .301, so he must have hit about .370 in the time I was there. He was still so graceful and such a good hitter, it made me realize how great he must have been in his prime.

As far as Mickey is concerned, there are so many memories of great things he did on the baseball field. But my greatest memories of him will always be the things we did off the field and the fun we had. And still have, because today Mick and I remain as close as we always were. He's the brother I never had.

After the 1955 season, the Yankees were invited to go to Japan on a goodwill tour. We were allowed to bring our wives, but Merlyn Mantle was pregnant, and she couldn't go.

In the first couple of days of the trip, we met this four-hundred-pound Sumo wrestler and we thought it would be fun to go out on the town with him. Through an interpreter we invited him to join us. So we went out, the four of us, Mickey, Billy Martin, me, and this Sumo wrestler. We were buying him drinks and having a good time and the wrestler hadn't said a word all night. All he did was smile whenever we said something or whenever we gave him another drink.

After a few hours we were getting pretty loaded, and Billy couldn't resist having some fun. There we were with this huge wrestler who didn't know what we were saying. So then Billy winked and handed the wrestler a drink and said, "You open your mouth and I'll knock you on your ass." And the wrestler just smiled and shook his head.

Then I would say something insulting. Again, the wrestler smiled and shook his head.

Now it was time to call it a night. Billy spoke a little Japanese, so he said good night to the wrestler in Japanese. And the guy just looked at us and said, as clear as day, "Well, good night, fellows. Thank you very much for a nice evening."

He spoke perfect English. Billy, Mickey, and I almost shit. The guy understood everything we had been saying and he was big enough to kill the three of us with his bare hands. Good thing he was a nice guy and he obviously had a sense of humor.

Mickey hated being in Japan. He complained all the time he was there. He was homesick and he was tired from the long season. He couldn't wait to get back to Commerce.

Then he got an idea. He had his business partner, Harold Youngman, have somebody back home send a cable to Japan:

MERLYN EXPECTING BABY ANY MINUTE. PLEASE GET HOME RIGHT AWAY.

Mantle showed the cable to Casey and Casey showed it to Commissioner Ford Frick.

"By all means," said Frick, "let him go home. His place is with his wife at a time like this."

So Mickey took the next plane home to Commerce. This was in October. The baby was born in January. We each got $3,500 to make the trip. When Mickey got his check, most of his money had been taken away from him in the form of a fine.

On the way back from Japan, we stopped off to play three games in Manila. One morning, while I was in the shower, Joan heard a knock on our hotel-room door. It was Billy, coming to pick me up to go to the ballpark. Joan was still in bed, but she got up to open the door, and when Billy walked in and realized I was in the shower, he got an idea. He crawled under the covers with Joan, clothes and all.

When I came out of the shower, the first thing I saw was somebody in bed with my wife. His back was to me, so I couldn't tell who it was.

"Hey, what's going on here?" I shouted.

Then the guy turned around and I saw it was Billy. I should have known.

At the time we were in Manila, the Philippines was about 35 percent Communist, and we were told to be very careful

102

because a lot of the natives didn't like Americans. One day Tom Sturdivant and his wife were going shopping and they asked Joan and me to join them. We were going to buy some linens because Manila is famous for its linens.

We took a cab and made the ten- or fifteen-mile trip into town, where we got out of the cab and started walking toward the shops. Just then, some old guy who looked to be about eighty came directly at us, pushing a cart full of melons. He made no attempt to avoid us and he would have run us over if we hadn't jumped out of the way. I knew it was intentional. I could hear him saying, in broken English, "American son of a bitch."

"Get away, you old bastard," I said.

I tried not to pay any attention to him, but he kept following us with his pushcart, yelling at us. Pretty soon a crowd had gathered and they had us encircled.

Sturdivant and I were getting a little nervous, to tell the truth, and our wives were scared to death. It was a good thing the cab driver hadn't left yet. He stepped into the middle of the circle and said, "Come on, we're going back to the hotel."

He didn't have to tell us twice.

That night, we got two detectives from the Manila police department to take the women shopping for their linens.

We played three day games in Manila in a little field, under a blistering sun. One thing that made an impression on me was a school building in right field. Painted on the bricks on the side of the building were signs that said: BABE RUTH HIT ONE HERE; LEFTY O'DOUL HIT ONE HERE; LOU GEHRIG HIT A HOME RUN HERE.

They had been there about twenty-five or thirty years earlier, when O'Doul and Ruth took a team of players to the Orient for the first time.

Another memorable experience came after the 1956 season when Mickey invited Billy and me to go hunting in Oklahoma. We stayed at Mickey's mother's house in Commerce, which was really a different experience for Billy and me. We had never seen a town as small as Commerce. If you saw the movie *The Last Picture Show,* you have an idea what Commerce is like. One theater. One gas station. A general store. A bank. One red light.

They took me quail hunting one day. It was the first time I had ever gone quail hunting. Hell, I had never even seen a quail before. The closest thing we had to quails in Astoria were the pigeons some guys flew from their roofs. I had never even fired a shotgun before.

But Mickey and Billy loved to hunt. So we went out just before dark and we came to a fence where the quail were all gathered around. The way Mickey explained it, it was winter and the wind was coming from the north and the quail liked to keep warm by gathering next to the fence. He called it a hedgerow. To me it was a fence with hedges on it. What did I know about a hedgerow? We didn't have too many of them in Astoria either.

Anyway, before we went out hunting, Mickey had explained how to hunt quail. The birds nest near the ground, and it's not sporting to shoot at them until they are in flight, then you pick them off one at a time. But when we came to that hedgerow (or whatever it was) full of quail, Billy just pulled up his shotgun and let them have it, right there huddled together. He must have shot ten quail with one blast!

The next morning, Mickey's mom woke us for breakfast and there was a delicious aroma coming from the kitchen. I went in and sat down and looked at my plate. There was something funny on it.

I didn't know it at the time, but it was the quail Billy had shot the day before. Mickey's mom had prepared it with homemade biscuits and gravy and it was delicious. Billy loved it. He must have gained twenty pounds on this trip. I liked it, too, but I never would have eaten quail for breakfast if it wasn't for Mickey. I wasn't used to things like quail for breakfast. I was used to Wheaties and ham and eggs.

There was a fellow in Commerce named Roy Crow. He was slightly retarded, but he was a nice, harmless guy who was loved by the whole town. Everybody tried to make him feel important. The bank gave him a bank book and a checking account and he'd get up every morning and make a deposit of 5 cents in his account, then he'd go to the store to buy an ice cream cone and he'd write out a check to pay for it.

Roy idolized Mickey. His whole life was coming to Mickey's house, wearing his Yankee cap, and sitting on the stoop and talking. He had a crush on Mickey's sister, Barbara, and Mickey used to like to tease him about it.

One day while we were there, Roy Crow showed up. I was in the kitchen with Mickey, and Billy was still asleep in the bedroom. Mickey began to tease Roy.

Roy called Billy "Bill Barton," and Mickey said to him, "You know, Roy, I think Barbara likes Bill Barton. I think he kissed her last night."

All of a sudden, Roy went storming through the house. He ran into the bedroom where Billy was fast asleep, jumped on the bed, and began pounding Billy on the chest. Billy didn't know what was going on except he'd awakened in a strange house and there was some guy pounding on his chest.

If you watched the 1986 World Series, and the ticker-tape parade down lower Broadway after the Mets won it, you got a good idea how even a supposedly cold and sophisticated city like New York goes crazy over baseball. You have to be in your fifties, or close to it, to appreciate what it was like when there were three major league teams in the city of New York, all within minutes of one another.

The rivalries were unbelievable. The Giants played in Manhattan, just over the bridge from Yankee Stadium. You could actually walk from one ballpark to the other. The Dodgers were in Brooklyn, about twenty or twenty-five miles away from both the Giants and the Yankees.

The city went wild when the Mets won the world championship because they hadn't won it in seventeen years. No New York team had won the World Series since the Yankees won it in 1978. And there hadn't been a World Series in New York in five years, since the Yankees lost to the Dodgers in 1981.

In the forties and fifties and into the early sixties, the World Series was in New York almost every year. In the twenty-four seasons from 1941 to 1964, New York had the World Series nineteen times, and it might have been more than that if World War II hadn't come along. From 1947 to 1964, New York was out of the Series only twice. And in the ten seasons from 1947 to 1956, two New York teams played against each other in the Series seven times.

The Dodgers and Giants were greater rivals because they played in the same league, but fans of both the Dodgers and Giants were united in their hatred of the Yankees because we used to win all the time.

No matter where you lived in the New York area, in any neighborhood there were always fans of all three local teams. Many of the people who lived in Queens were folks who moved from Manhattan or the Bronx, and they brought with them their loyalties to their baseball team. Generally, the older folks, our fathers and grandfathers, were Giants fans going back to the

John McGraw days, when the Giants were a perennial power. A lot of the younger people adopted the Dodgers when they began to get good in the forties.

When I was a kid growing up in Astoria, we would stand in the street outside the local candy store arguing into the night who was better, Joe DiMaggio, Mel Ott of the Giants, or Pete Reiser of the Dodgers. Later, it was who was better, Pee Wee Reese or Phil Rizzuto; Roy Campanella or Yogi Berra; Mickey Mantle, Willie Mays, or Duke Snider.

Unless you lived through it, you can't imagine what a baseball-mad city New York was in the fifties. The rivalries were intense, the loyalties fierce.

As a player, you couldn't help get caught up in the rivalry, especially between the Yankees and Dodgers. The best thing for us was to get on that team bus and drive to Ebbets Field. We'd drive through Brooklyn and it seemed everybody in Brooklyn knew the bus was coming by. They'd have signs up knocking the Yankees and they'd be standing there booing us and yelling things at us when we stopped for a red light.

I loved it. I thought it was great. The enthusiasm was unbelievable and it just carried over to the players. We especially loved it because we usually beat the Dodgers and we got a great pleasure out of kicking their ass and shutting up their fans.

I had some good friends on the Dodgers and it wasn't the players so much that made us want to beat them. Of course, we wanted to win, but we got our pleasure out of shutting up those loud fans.

I never pitched well in Ebbets Field because it was such a tiny ballpark with a short fence in left field and the Dodgers tailored their team to it. They had all those big right-handed power hitters like Gil Hodges, Roy Campanella, Carl Furillo,

Jackie Robinson, and Andy Pafko. Even guys like Billy Cox and Pee Wee Reese, not normally known as power hitters, were threats in their little ballpark, and they gave me fits there. I pitched my best games against the Dodgers in Yankee Stadium, where I could use the spacious left-center field, the so-called Death Valley, to my advantage. The Dodgers used to get so frustrated hitting those four-hundred-foot shots that would have been home runs in their park, and watching Joe D. or Mick go back and catch them easily.

We always felt we could beat the Dodgers, that they would never beat us in the World Series. That's because the Yankees had beaten them in the Series in 1941, 1947, 1949, 1952, and 1953. It was like we had their number. But in 1955 the Dodgers finally won one.

Vic Raschi, Allie Reynolds, Eddie Lopat, and Johnny Sain were all gone by 1955. Our entire starting pitching corps had to be revamped and we had acquired Bob Turley and Don Larsen in trades. Tommy Byrne came back from the minor leagues to win sixteen games. And we had a couple of newcomers, Bob Grim and Johnny Kucks.

I led the staff in wins with eighteen (I lost seven), and I was named to pitch the opener of the 1955 Series in Yankee Stadium against Don Newcombe.

Mantle had a bad leg and didn't play the first two games of the Series, but Joe Collins hit two home runs in the first game and I took a 6–3 lead into the eighth.

Then the Dodgers rallied for two runs to make it 6–5, but they never should have scored the fifth run. I'll never believe they did score it. That was the controversial play in which Jackie Robinson stole home with pinch hitter Frank Kellert at bat.

When Jackie reached third, I knew he was going to try to steal home. I wasn't worried. I almost dared him to by taking a long windup as he danced off the bag. Sure enough, he took off for the plate and I threw the ball to Yogi and got it there in plenty of time. The pitch was low, right where I wanted it, and Yogi just caught it and put his mitt down on the ground in front of the plate and Robinson slid right into the tag. Robinson was out, there was no question about it. But the plate umpire, Bill Summers, was a little guy, shorter than Yogi, and he was blocked out of the play. He was just too short to see over Yogi's head. If you watch the films, you'll see that Summers was in no position to make the call.

Summers called Robinson safe and Yogi, who rarely argued with an umpire, went wild. He started jumping up and down, yelling at Summers that he blew the call. We all started yelling, but it was no use.

To this day, I still believe that Jackie was out. I've seen the films of that play maybe fifty times, and Robinson is out every time.

I finished the inning and Casey brought in Grim to pitch the ninth and nail down the 6–5 victory. We won the second game, too, with Byrne beating my old buddy Billy Loes, and we were ahead in the Series, two games to none. No team had ever come back to win the World Series after losing the first two games, so we were confident we were going to win it again. We were even thinking sweep. After all, we had the Dodgers' number, didn't we?

But the Dodgers were a different team in their ballpark, and they won the next three games in Ebbets Field to take a 3-2 lead. Now we were the ones with our backs to the wall.

I was scheduled to pitch the sixth game to try to keep us alive. I also was scheduled to appear on the *Ed Sullivan Show.*

The *Ed Sullivan Show* was the big television event in those days. Ed was a former sportswriter who became a Broadway

columnist for the New York *Daily News* and then started doing this variety show on television. It was the first show of its
kind. Everybody watched the *Ed Sullivan Show* because his
guests were always the biggest names in entertainment. He
also used to invite the biggest names in sports to make an
appearance.

The show was live on Sunday night, which was the night of
the fifth game that year. There were no days off in the World
Series back then, so Game Six, in Yankee Stadium, was the
next day. Mickey Mantle, Tommy Byrne, and I had committed
ourselves to appear on the show, so we did it even though
none of us was in the mood to go there after we lost the
fifth game.

Normally, whatever sports people Ed had would just sit in
the audience; Ed would introduce them, and they would stand
up and take a bow. That was it. But this time, because everybody was talking about the World Series, Ed invited us up to
the stage and talked to us for a few minutes.

"Who's pitching tomorrow's game?" Ed asked.

"I am," I said. "And Tommy's pitching the seventh game."

I didn't mean it the way it sounded and I realize now that
was a pretty cocky-sounding thing for me to say, like I was
boasting that I would see to it that there would be a seventh
game. A lot of people around the country heard me and I think
that's one of the reasons I got the reputation of being a cocky
fellow.

Fortunately for me, I did win the sixth game. We scored five
runs off Karl Spooner in the first, knocking him out of the game,
and even though that's all we scored, I made it stand up. I
gave them a run in the fourth, then held them the rest of the
way, and won, 5–1, on a four-hitter.

Now the Series was tied and I was confident that Byrne

would beat them in the seventh game and we'd be world champs again.

Tommy pitched a great game, but that was the game of the famous catch by Sandy Amoros. The Dodgers were leading, 2–0, in the bottom of the sixth when we got our first two men on base and had Yogi Berra coming up.

The Dodgers had just made a defensive change in that inning, which proved to be the turning point of the game. They put Amoros in left field in place of Junior Gilliam, who moved to second base. The reason it was such a critical move was that Amoros was a left-handed thrower and he had his glove on his right hand. A right-handed thrower never could have done what Sandy did.

Yogi hit a slicing drive down the left-field line. Amoros had great speed and he ran a long way to catch up to the ball (another important factor). He reached the ball just as it was about to drop inside the left-field line, stuck out his glove, and the ball landed right in the glove. As I said, if he had had his glove on his left hand, he never would have been able to make the catch.

Our two runners, Billy Martin on second and Gil McDougald on first, were sure the ball would drop, and they started running with the crack of the bat. In one motion, Amoros caught the ball, spun around, and fired to shortstop Pee Wee Reese, who relayed to first baseman Gil Hodges in time to double up McDougald.

That play was a rally killer and a backbreaker. We had a few more shots at Johnny Podres, who was a surprise starter in the seventh game because he had won only nine games during the regular season, but he was tough with men on base. We got eight hits off Podres, but we couldn't get the hit when we needed it and he beat us, 2–0.

Not only was it the Dodgers' first world championship in their history, they had finally broken the jinx against the hated Yankees, who had beaten them in their five previous World Series matchups.

We vowed to avenge that defeat.

We didn't have to wait long for our chance to avenge ourselves against the Dodgers. They won their pennant in 1956 by one game over Milwaukee, and we won by nine games over Cleveland, and we met again in the World Series.

I was 19-6 for the season and Stengel picked me to pitch the Series opener, even though it was in Brooklyn. Again, I was afflicted with the Ebbets Field curse. Jackie Robinson homered in the second. Gil Hodges hit a three-run homer in the third. And I left for a pinch hitter in the top of the fourth, trailing 5–2. The Dodgers went on to win the game, 6–3.

Casey started Don Larsen in the second game against Don Newcombe. Neither of them could get past the second inning, and the Dodgers wound up winning a slugfest, 13–8.

Now we went back home trailing, two games to none, just as the Dodgers had the year before. We told ourselves if they could come back and win from that deficit in 1955, why couldn't we do the same in 1956? It was up to me to get us started because Casey was bringing me back in Game Three with two days' rest. I got batting support from Billy Martin and Enos (Country) Slaughter, who both hit home runs, and won the game, 5–3.

Tommy Sturdivant beat them, 6–2, in the fourth game, and now we were all tied up, two games apiece.

Game Five was played on Monday, October 8, a typical Indian summer afternoon in New York, with blue skies, brilliant sun, and a nip in the air. The pitching matchup was an interesting and curious one. The Dodgers went with thirty-nine-year-old Sal Maglie, "The Barber," who was a story in himself. Maglie was a Dodger killer when he pitched for the Giants in the early fifties, one of the most hated men in Brooklyn. As fate would have it, the hated one would wind up with the Dodgers and become one of their most beloved players.

Thinking that Maglie's best days were behind him, the Giants sold him to Cleveland in 1955 for the waiver price. He hadn't won a game for the Indians when the Dodgers, desperate for pitching, bought him on May 15, 1956.

Maglie became a lifesaver for the Dodgers, who wouldn't have won the pennant without him. He won thirteen games for them, including a no-hitter, and lost only five, and he was their opening-game pitcher in the 1956 World Series. He was the winner in the game I lost.

Stengel shocked everybody when he chose for his starting pitcher in the important fifth game journeyman Don Larsen, whose story was even more bizarre than Maglie's.

Larsen had come to us with Bob Turley after the 1954 season as part of a trade with the St. Louis Browns. He had won ten games and lost thirty-three in two seasons with the Browns, but he became a useful pitcher for us. He was 9-2 in 1955 and 11-5 in 1956. But he had failed to survive the second inning in Game Two and nobody expected him to be pitching the fifth game.

There was a lot of speculation in the press over who Stengel would choose to pitch the fifth game, but Larsen's name never came up. Casey never explained why he selected him and Larsen never told anybody how he spent the night before the game. Because of his reputation, the word got around that he stayed up all night partying. Knowing Don, it was believable.

Larsen was one of the most misunderstood players I've ever played with. Sure, he loved to party, and he was a pretty good drinker. But he was one of the most decent and nicest men I knew and his reputation for being a party guy obscured the fact that he was a damn good pitcher and a great competitor.

On that trip to Japan after the 1955 season, we stopped off in Hawaii. Before the trip continued, we had to get shots and all the pitchers took them in their nonpitching arms because the shots hurt and there was a possible negative reaction from them.

One night Joan and I went out to dinner and then to one of the local clubs. It was about two or three in the morning when we returned to the Royal Hawaiian Hotel, and just as we arrived, Larsen pulled up in a cab and started zigging and zagging up the steps of the hotel, heading for the lobby.

"Hey, Gooney Bird," I shouted. "How you doing?"

And Don just turned around and said, "You'd drink, too, if you got those shots," which made me laugh, because Don never needed an excuse to take a drink.

Another time, a bunch of couples got together during spring training and went to Miami Beach to see Frank Sinatra perform. Larsen was one of the single guys who came along. He sat down at the table and the first thing he did was order a beer. Then he had a rum and Coke. Then he ordered a Scotch and soda. Then he had Canadian Club. I never saw anybody mix drinks like that.

All of a sudden, Don got a case of the hiccups. He couldn't stop them, so he got up from the table and went to the kitchen, got a shot of vinegar, slugged the vinegar down, and the hiccups just stopped.

I mentioned that Larsen's nickname was Gooney Bird. That

was because he did some strange things. I'll give you an example.

It was the last weekend of the 1955 season and we were playing in Boston. We needed one victory to clinch the pennant and Larsen started for us and pitched a terrific game. We were leading 4–1 in the eighth inning when the Red Sox rallied. They had runners on second and third with one out and Billy Goodman and Ted Williams due up.

I had been sent down to the bullpen to warm up just in case a situation like this arose. It was rare for me to be brought in to relieve in Fenway Park, but with two left-handed hitters coming up, Casey removed Larsen and brought me in.

"We'll try to get this fella [Goodman] out," Stengel told me, "then we'll walk Williams and pitch to the next guy."

Instead, I walked Goodman to load the bases, and here came Ted Williams, the winning run. If he hit a home run, we would be behind, 5–4. I went 3-and-1 on him and now I was in danger of walking him. I didn't want to walk Williams and keep the rally going, but I didn't want him to hit a home run either.

"What the hell," I said to myself, and I threw a mediocre fastball right down the middle. Most times, Williams would hit that ball out of sight. This time, I got lucky. He hit it hard, but right at second baseman Billy Martin, a perfect two-hopper, and Billy started a double play to get us out of the inning.

Jackie Jensen hit a home run in the ninth with nobody on, but I got them out and we won the game, 4–2, clinching the pennant.

Then I came off the field and headed right for the clubhouse. In those days, when a big game was over, we headed right for the clubhouse. We didn't spend ten minutes shaking hands as they do today.

I went into the clubhouse and was looking around for Larsen. I wanted to congratulate him for winning the clincher, and I expected him to be waiting to thank me for saving the game for him. But there was no Larsen.

I finally found him in the room next to the shower. They used to keep big blocks of ice in the room, and there was Gooney Bird sitting on a block of ice, drinking a beer. He was still dressed in his uniform. He was so nervous, he couldn't listen to the end of the game, so he grabbed a beer and turned all the showers on full blast so he couldn't hear the radio that was playing in the clubhouse, and he sat down on a cake of ice with his fingers in his ears. He didn't even know we had won the game, and the pennant, until I came in and told him.

A year later it was the fifth game of the 1956 World Series, and Larsen was pitching the biggest game of his life. Mantle hit a home run off Maglie in the fourth for a 1–0 lead and Hank Bauer singled in a run in the sixth to make it 2–0.

Meanwhile, Larsen was pitching the game of his life. Through six innings, to everybody's amazement, he hadn't allowed a hit. He hadn't even allowed a base runner.

Where was I while all this was going on? In the bullpen again. Jim Turner, our pitching coach, had sent me down.

"Go down there and be ready," Turner said, "because we never know how many innings we're going to get out of this guy. We may need you."

I watched the first two innings from the dugout, then I went down to the bullpen in the third. In the sixth, as Larsen went out to pitch, Turner called down to the bullpen and told me to start loosening up.

I started throwing easily, but Larsen got them one-two-three, so I sat down. Then, when the seventh inning started, they called down again and I started loosening up again, and Larsen got them out one-two-three again. I loosened up at the start of every inning for the final four innings, but, of course, I never was needed.

You know what happened. Larsen pitched the greatest game in baseball history that day. It was the only no-hitter ever pitched in the World Series. Not only that, it was a perfect game, twenty-seven batters up, twenty-seven batters retired. You can't do better than that.

I never did see the game. I would stop during my warm-ups and try to look at the game, but you couldn't see anything from the bullpen. All I could see was the shortstop and the third baseman. So between warming up, and not being able to see the field, I missed the greatest pitching performance in baseball history, and I had to rely on the cheers of the crowd to tell me what was going on.

Everybody was shocked at what Larsen did. "The imperfect man pitched the perfect game," one newspaper said. And I guess nobody was more shocked than Gooney Bird himself.

We went back to Brooklyn leading, three games to two, but the Dodgers won the sixth game when Clem Labine beat Bob Turley, 1–0, on Jackie Robinson's one-out single in the tenth inning. Turley allowed four hits and struck out eleven and lost. Labine allowed seven hits, struck out five, and won.

Now we were tied, three games apiece, and the seventh game was in Ebbets Field, and everybody was speculating again on who Casey was going to start in the final game.

I knew it wasn't going to be me for two reasons—my record in Ebbets Field and the fact that I had warmed up for four innings during Larsen's game.

Casey came up with another surprise. He chose Johnny Kucks, who had won eighteen games during the regular season, but who hadn't started a game during the World Series. Kucks was brilliant. He shut the Dodgers out on three hits. Yogi hit a pair of homers off Don Newcombe, Moose Skowron hit a grand slam, and Ellie Howard also homered, and we won, 10–0. We had avenged the World Series defeat to the Dodgers the year before.

After the final game, Joan and I went to a party at a little nightclub in Glen Cove. It was about 1:30 in the morning and this guy came over to say hello. His name was Denny Slater. Denny was the president of the Fanny Farmer candy company. I had known him casually, but we weren't really good friends.

Denny lived in Locust Valley, a very fancy section of Long Island, and he invited us to his house.

"There's a party going on," he said. "I'd like you to come and join us because there are some people I'd like you to meet."

Joan and I went with him, and so did Joan's sister, Sally, and her husband, Tommy Slattery. The party was still in full swing. When we arrived Denny Slater left us to go upstairs. He came down a few minutes later with a man and a woman. I looked at them and I said to myself, "Damn, they look familiar."

The man was a skinny little guy. He was wearing his bathrobe, but he was very elegant. The woman also was wearing a bathrobe. Suddenly, it occurred to me who they were. The Duke and Duchess of Windsor!

The Duke said hello, then excused himself and went back to bed. But the Duchess went upstairs to change into a dress, then came back to join the party. The next thing you knew, we were in the kitchen and the Duchess was making sandwiches for us.

She was a lovely, classy woman. She remembered that we had met once before when she and the Duke visited Yankee Stadium and they posed for pictures with Casey Stengel, Johnny Mize, Gil McDougald, and me.

My mom and me in Central Park.
Whitey Ford Collection

I tease my two grand-
sons now because they
have their hair cut this
way.
Whitey Ford Collection

My first lifeguard job in
Lake Ronkonkama,
N.Y.
Whitey Ford Collection

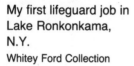

New York City sandlot champs: Top row, from left to right—Oakley, Stumpf, Cavanaugh, Lefty Willman (manager), Derle, Cashman, Bischoff. Bottom row, from left—Burbes, me, Martin (not Billy), Shortell, Perduto.
courtesy *Yankees Magazine*

Opposite: My biggest fan, Grandma Johnson, in our city condominium. You can tell from the skyline that we didn't live in the country.
Whitey Ford Collection

With the Mazatlán Rein-
deers in Mexico. Six weeks
after this picture was taken,
Montezuma had his revenge
and my weight dropped to
140.

Whitey Ford Collection

My high, hard(?) one.
National Baseball Library, Cooperstown, N.Y.

Opposite: Casey telling me to stay away from Martin and Mantle.
AP/Wide World

This is the high-priced barnstorming team that went to Hawaii and ended up playing for nothing when the promoter skipped town with our money. Top row, from left: clubhouse attendant Herb Norman, Hank Sauer, Harvey Kuenn, Sammy White, Del Crandall, Bob Grimm, Carl Erskine, agent Frank Scott. Bottom row: me, Irv Noren, Red Schoendienst, Billy Goodman, Duke Snider.
Whitey Ford Collection

Ralph Houk, Yogi, and me. I had just been named pitching coach for the 1964 season by Berra, the new manager. Little did we know at the time that we were both going to be fired after one season. At least I could stay on as a pitcher.
Bob Olen Studios, courtesy *Yankees Magazine*

With Moose Skowron after he hit a home run in the opening game of the 1961 World Series to beat Jim O'Toole, 2–0.
Bob Olen Studios, courtesy *Yankees Magazine*

These were the fun times in
Fort Lauderdale, Florida, during spring training. We were
staying at the Galt Ocean
Mile Hotel. That's Eddie on
the left, Sally Ann, and
Tommy sitting in front of Joan
and me.
Whitey Ford Collection

Eddie, Sally Ann, me, and
Tommy with one of their toys.
The kids knew that if they
ever broke a toy, their father
could never fix it, so they
were very careful.
UPI/Bettmann Newsphotos

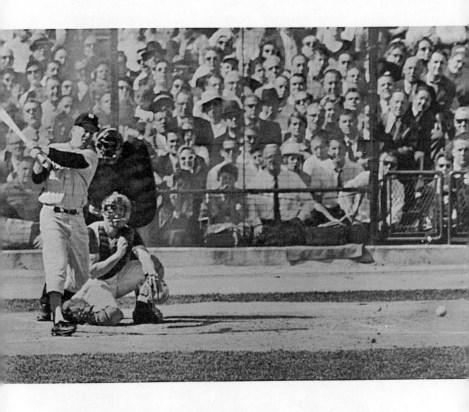

A rare picture. Me getting a base hit off the Pirates' Bob Friend in the sixth game of the 1960 World Series.
AP/Wide World

Opposite: The two catchers who caught me my whole career, Elston Howard, left, and Yogi Berra, right. It was Ellie who dubbed me "The Chairman of the Board."
AP/Wide World

Me, Billy Martin, and Mickey Mantle at Al Lang
Field in St. Petersburg. Billy was scouting for the
Twins at the time and we had one of our get to-
gethers, rare after he left the Yankees.
Whitey Ford Collection

This is my favorite picture. With General Douglas MacArthur,
taken at the General's seventy-fifth-birthday party at the Waldorf-
Astoria in 1955.
Whitey Ford Collection

Joan and me at Yankee Stadium three days after our wedding! The Yankees had asked me to throw out the first ball on Opening Day of the 1951 season.
UPI/Bettmann Newsphotos

Two of my biggest fans, my mom on the left and my Grandma Johnson, who knew more baseball than anybody in the family. They had just appeared on Red Barber's postgame show.
AP/Wide World

Pitchers come in all sizes, shapes, and speeds. Here are a super fastball pitcher, Allie Reynolds, a medium-speed pitcher, me, and a very slow pitcher, Eddie Lopat.
National Baseball Library, Cooperstown, N.Y.

Mickey, Bobby Richardson, and me after the third game of the 1960 World Series. Mickey had four hits includin a home run, Bobby drove in six runs, and I pitched a fou hit shutout.
AP/Wide World

The guy sitting on the cart, on the right, is Jackie Gleason. I had just beaten him for the "World Golf Championship." The big trophy is mine. The little one held by Tommy Strafaci is "The Great One's" consolation prize. Also in the picture are Jack Philbin (standing, left) and Jim Tsunis (sitting on left in cart).
Whitey Ford Collection

Elio Chacon grounding out to Bobby Richardson for the third out in the third inning of the fourth game of the 1961 World Series. With that out, I broke Babe Ruth's World Series record of 29⅔ consecutive scoreless innings.
UPI/Bettmann Newsphotos

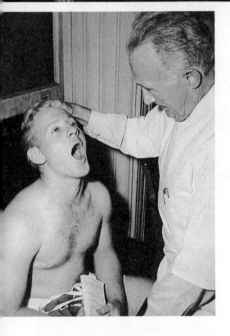

Whitey Ford Day, September
9, 1961. I tried not to show
how much it meant to me, but
that didn't last for long.
National Baseball Library,
Cooperstown, N.Y.

Top: With three of my good buddies, left to
right, Kyle Rote, Eddie Arcaro, and Toots
Shor, at the New York baseball writers'
dinner.
Bill Mark, N.Y.C.

Above: The army finds me physically fit
and in good enough shape to defend my
country from Fort Monmouth, N.J.
UPI/Bettmann Newsphotos

September 1946. I receive the
Lou Gehrig award from Rabbit
Maranville for being the MVP in
the *Journal-American* game.
UPI/Bettmann Newsphotos

Twenty-four years later, my son
Eddie receives the same award.
Dan Farrell/*New York Daily News*

A sad day. My official retire-
ment from the Yankees,
May 30, 1967.
Rochester Times Union

Left to right, Mickey Mantle, Casey Stengel, and me.
One of my biggest thrills, getting into the Hall of Fame
with my buddy Mickey. Casey was there to share it with
us—our proudest day.
National Baseball Library, Cooperstown, N.Y.

With my good buddy, harness racing
Hall of Famer Del Miller, at a rodeo in
Fort Lauderdale.
Whitey Ford Collection

Hank Aaron and me. We had 758
home runs between us. I hit them all
except for 755. I asked Hank to pose
for this picture with me because we
have something in common. We both
hit our first home run off the same
pitcher, my old teammate Vic Raschi.
Whitey Ford Collection

We didn't leave the party until about four in the morning. When we got home, Joan's mother was waiting up for us. She had been baby sitting for our children. Of course, we were excited about the evening and we wanted to share our recent thrill with her.

"Mom," Joan said, "guess who we met tonight? The Duke and Duchess of Windsor."

Joan's mother speaks with a thick Scottish brogue. She just looked at us and said, "Go on, you're both daft, the two of you."

That winter, I went on my usual round of parties and dinners. One of the dinners was the annual New York baseball writers' shindig. I attended that dinner, then we all went over to Toots Shor's after the dinner for a few drinks. I got home at seven in the morning.

We were living in Glen Cove at the time and we used to have to bring our garbage cans down to the street for collection. I figured as long as I was up, I'd save Joan the trouble and I'd put the garbage cans out. I made such a racket with the cans, I woke Joan. She looked out the window to see what all the noise was about, and there I was, in my tuxedo, weaving my way down the driveway with the garbage cans. The neighbors were going to work and they saw me in a tuxedo putting the garbage cans on the curb. Joan was mortified. She was so mad, she wouldn't talk to me.

I went to bed about 7:30 and I got up at 4:00 in the afternoon and started getting dressed.

"Where are you going now?" Joan said.

I told her that I had received a call from Frank Farrell, who was a Broadway columnist for the old *New York World-Telegram and Sun,* inviting me to a seventy-fifth-birthday party for General Douglas MacArthur at the Waldorf-Astoria.

"You're invited, too," I said.

"What are you, trying to be cute?" Joan said. "Where are you going?"

"I told you, I'm going to General MacArthur's seventy-fifth-birthday party. Why don't you come with me?"

"Oh, why don't you stop it with your wild stories?"

So, I went off to the party without her and the next day in the paper there was a picture of me and General MacArthur and he's holding my arm. A picture I'm very proud of. To this day it hangs on the wall of my den.

"You louse," Joan said. "How did I know you were telling the truth? I thought you were kidding. I thought you were going to another of your baseball dinners."

"Well," I said smugly, "you can't say I didn't invite you to come along."

It was the next year that Mickey, Billy, and I came to an end as the "Unholy Trio" of the Yankees. It happened in the middle of the 1957 season as a direct result of the "Copa Incident." You may have heard about this, when several Yankees were supposed to have been in a fight with some guys at the Copacabana nightclub. I don't know what you heard, but this is exactly what happened.

It was a Sunday and Mickey and I had planned a birthday party for Billy that night after the game. Monday was a day off, so we could stay out a little later Sunday night. We invited most of the older guys to come. There was Yogi Berra, Hank Bauer, Gil McDougald, Johnny Kucks, and me, plus all of our wives. And Mickey and Billy, who came stag.

We didn't even plan to go to the Copa. We arranged to have dinner at Danny's Hide-a-way and after dinner, it was still early, and we wanted to continue our birthday party. It was Danny Stradella, the owner of Danny's Hide-a-way, who suggested we go to the Copa. He had a table there and he told us we were welcome to use it.

It sounded like a good idea, so off we all went to the Copa to catch Sammy Davis, Jr.'s last show.

There was another group not too far from us sitting at a big, long table. It turned out it was a bowling team and they had been there several hours. That was obvious because they were pretty well juiced and they were making a lot of noise. They started calling Sammy Davis "Sambo" and making other racial remarks like that.

Bauer yelled over to them to cool it, in a nice way, not hostile. But the next thing we knew, one of the guys said, "Who's going to make me?"

Then he got up and it looked like he and Bauer were going to get into it. They walked to a room in the back and the rest of us got up and followed, just in case.

The guy who said that to Hank got to the back room before any of us, even Hank. All of a sudden, we heard a crash and by the time we got there, the guy was stretched out on the floor. My eyes never left Hank, so I know he didn't do it. And Billy was right next to me all the time, so I know he didn't do it. And I know I didn't do it. To this day, I don't know who slugged the guy. I think it was one of the Copa bouncers because it was a real professional job.

I knew one thing: We had to get out of there fast. If it hit the papers, we'd be in deep trouble. One of the bouncers must have realized the same thing because he led us out of the place through an exit in the rear. Joan says she never knew what happened, just that she and the other wives were being ushered out of the Copa through the kitchen into the lobby of a hotel next to the nightclub. When we had assembled in the hotel lobby, we all went to our cars and went home.

The next morning I got a call from Mickey and Billy, telling me that George Weiss wanted to see us in his office at eleven. We were going to be fined $1,000 each. It was already ten and I lived at least an hour away from the Yankees' offices. There was no way I could make it there by eleven, so I decided just not to go. (They threatened to add another $1,000 for that. I was so pissed off.)

"I'm not coming," I said. "Do whatever you want. I'm staying home."

Mickey and Billy went and told exactly what happened. The next day, Dan Topping got his lawyer, and he met in Topping's office with all the guys involved.

"Tell me exactly what happened," the lawyer said.

We told the story one more time, exactly as it happened.

"Fine," the lawyer said. "Tell that story to the grand jury just like you told me."

And that was it. We were with the guy an hour and all he told us to do was tell the same story to the grand jury. The guy sent us a bill for $6,500, which was almost another $1,000 each. So, between the fine and the lawyer's fee, it cost us $2,000 apiece for doing nothing. The grand jury even threw the case out.

At the grand jury hearing, I remember Mantle standing in the middle of the room, giving his testimony. There was no chair, nothing. He was standing there and chewing gum and one of the jurors asked him, "What are you chewing, Mr. Mantle?"

"Gum," Mick said.

"Would you mind taking it out of your mouth?"

Mick took the gum out of his mouth and there was no place to put it, so he had to hold it in his hand for the rest of the time he was being questioned.

SLICK

George Weiss never should have fined us in the first place. We were with our wives and we had no game the next day. I never cared for Weiss after that and I was with him a long time. Especially after the grand jury threw out the case, he should have apologized to us and returned the money, but he never did. We were innocent, but I don't think he ever believed that.

At first Bauer was blamed because the guy said it was Hank that hit him. Then the story got around that it was Billy who hit him. Believe me, neither of them did it. The guy was lying on the ground when we got there.

I think Weiss made Billy the scapegoat because he never liked him and he was looking for an excuse to get rid of him. The funny thing is, the whole thing had nothing to do with Billy. He didn't do a thing. He didn't even organize the party; Mickey and I did that. It just happened to be Billy's birthday, that's all.

Exactly a month to the day after the Copa Incident, Billy was traded to Kansas City. It was no coincidence.

A week after that, I was pitching against Kansas City and we were leading by about eight or nine runs. It was the eighth inning and Billy came to bat. I threw him a big slow curve and he took it for a strike. I got the ball back and said to him, "Same thing." I wanted him to hit it for a single or a double, but I threw another big slow curve and he wrapped it around the left-field foul pole for a home run. Now he was prancing around the bases, the son of a bitch. When I saw him prancing like that, I was sorry I did it.

Casey must have heard me say something to Billy because when I got to our dugout after the inning, he said to me, "Did you tell that guy what was coming?" He wouldn't even mention Billy by name.

"No, Case," I said.

"You said something out there."

"It had nothing to do with the game."

The last thing Casey wanted was to be shown up by a player he had just traded away.

Sometimes, we went a couple of years without seeing Billy because soon after being traded, he went to the National League, then he scouted for a few years, then he managed in the minor leagues. So it was just Mickey and me after Billy was traded.

One time in 1963 we were playing in Baltimore. It was a Saturday and I had pitched that day and Mickey was just about to come off the disabled list. He and Merlyn had these friends from Dallas who had just bought a farm outside of Baltimore and they invited us over to spend the day. Since neither of us expected to be playing the next day, we went.

We had dinner with them and then we started drinking. The next thing you knew, Mickey had fallen asleep on the porch. We both got up at dawn and I drove Mickey straight to the ballpark; there was no time to even go back to the hotel. I got Mickey into the shower, then into the whirlpool. Finally I got him to lie down for a while to sleep, but he was still in pretty bad shape when the game started.

Our old teammate Hank Bauer, who was now coaching for the Orioles, noticed Mickey in batting practice and he couldn't believe what he saw. He made some comment to Mickey about how he looked.

"It's all right," Mickey told Hank. "I'm not playing today."

When the game started, Mickey took a seat on the far side of the dugout, as far away from our current manager, Ralph Houk, as he could get. He put on sunglasses and fell asleep on the bench.

SLICK

Then it was the ninth inning. Mike McCormick was pitching for the Orioles and we were behind. All of a sudden I saw Houk heading our way and I knew what he was going to do.

I shook Mickey, "Wake up, wake up, Houk's coming."

Sure enough, Houk came down and said to Mickey, "Can you hit?"

"I'm not eligible," Mickey said. "I'm on the disabled list."

"No you're not," Houk said. "You went on the active list today."

I think Mickey's heart stopped for a minute. Anyway, he had no choice. He couldn't tell Houk he was hung over, so he reached for his hat, which I was sitting on. He put it on his head and it was all rumpled. Then he went to the bat rack for a bat and I told him, "Hit the first pitch you see."

When Mickey went up to the plate, I saw Bauer talking to the Orioles' manager, Billy Hitchcock. Then Hitchcock sent Bauer out to the mound to talk to McCormick.

He must have said something to McCormick like "This guy's hung over. Don't throw him a strike; he can't see the ball."

McCormick's first pitch was head high and Mickey swung and hit it over the fence.

I looked over at the Orioles' bench and there was Bauer looking like he wanted to find a hole and crawl into it. Mickey was running around the bases and Hank was cursing him and I was laughing like hell.

Mickey got back to the bench and sat down next to me.

"Hitting the ball was easy," Mickey said. "Running around the bases was the tough part."

CHAPTER 5

Things were different after the Dodgers and Giants left town and moved to California following the 1957 season. It was as if the heart had been taken out of New York baseball.

You might figure that the Yankees would benefit from the Dodgers and Giants leaving, since it meant we were the only wheel in town. Not so. Our attendance actually dropped the year they left and we picked up only about 100,000 the second year they were gone, even though we continued to win. When we won the American League pennant in 1958, it gave us four pennants in a row and nine in the previous ten years.

All our falling attendance proved was that baseball thrived on the intercity competition between the Yankees and Dodgers, the Yankees and Giants, and the Dodgers and Giants. There were no more arguments on street corners about who was better, Mantle, Mays, or Snider, and as a result, interest waned.

In the four seasons from 1957 to 1960, my record was a combined 53-31, which meant I averaged twelve wins and eight losses a year, which wasn't very good. Part of the problem was a series of nagging injuries that caused me to miss several starts each year, and we were still operating on Stengel's five-day rotation. There was even some speculation that I was nearing the end of the line, even though I was just into my thirties, which are supposed to be the peak years for a pitcher.

In the 1957 World Series, our opponents had been the Milwaukee Braves, who had a powerful lineup that included Henry Aaron, Eddie Mathews, Joe Adcock, Andy Pafko, and Wes Covington. Casey named me to be his Game One pitcher against the Braves in 1957.

A lot of people have asked me what went through my mind before a big game. Did I think about it? Worry about it? Lose sleep over it? Dream about it?

I can honestly say that I never had trouble sleeping the night before a big game. And only once did I dream about the upcoming game. I dreamed I hit a home run off Sandy Koufax in the bottom of the ninth inning to win the seventh game of the World Series. Me hit a home run off Sandy Koufax? You know that had to be a dream.

I always approached every game the same way, whether it was the seventh game of the World Series or a regular-season game in June.

I never had any problems sleeping the night before a game, at least not because I was thinking about the game. If we were home for about two weeks, I'd be in a routine and I'd always get my proper rest, except that when the kids were little, they'd usually wake me up early. It was the first night after flying from one coast to the other that sleeping was a problem, but because of the jet lag, not because the game was on my mind.

On the road, I always got to bed early on the night before I was scheduled to pitch. I was very serious about that. On the other nights, I might go out, but on the night before I pitched, I always made sure I got my proper rest, about seven or eight hours of sleep. To this day, Mickey Mantle still talks about what a drag I was. I was no fun to be with the night before I pitched.

The Yankees must not have thought so because in the 1958 season we were going bad and the club hired a private detective to follow us. It wasn't meant just for me, it was meant for all of us, and it got ridiculous at times.

This guy was no Mike Hammer. He wore white rabbit-skin shoes and you could spot him a mile away. Some detective! We would do funny things to drive this guy crazy. We'd walk out one door of the Statler Hotel in Detroit, get in a cab, and have the driver go around the corner and park in front of another entrance to the hotel. The detective would be looking all over for us.

One night he followed Tony Kubek, Bobby Shantz, and Bobby Richardson, who were three of the cleanest-living players we had. None of them drank. Bobby, especially, was very religious, but he never wore his religion on his sleeve. We all respected him for it and he was one of the most liked players on the team.

Our detective didn't know that and this one night Kubek, Shantz, and Richardson left the hotel and the detective followed them. They walked several blocks through the streets of Detroit, the detective trailing them every step of the way.

He followed them right to the local YMCA, where they had gone to play Ping-Pong.

My pitching routine was always the same. If I pitched on a Sunday, say, the next day I'd come to the ballpark and I wouldn't do very much.

I might go to the outfield during batting practice and just throw the ball a little. I'd throw easily and I'd throw long to stretch out my arm.

The second day I would work hard. I would warm up good before the game, or late in the game I might go to the bullpen and throw hard for about twenty minutes or a half hour. Then I'd run sprints in the outfield. I'd get a vigorous workout.

On the third day, I did nothing, maybe just shagged balls in the outfield.

Then, on the fourth day, I'd be ready to pitch.

If I was on a five-day rotation, I would do my hard throwing and running on the third day instead of the second.

I usually didn't start thinking seriously about the game and how I was going to pitch the hitters until about noon on the day of an afternoon game. The two hours before I started warming up to pitch were always the worst for me. I'd go over the hitters in my mind and the butterflies would start. When I started warming up I calmed down. Then, when I faced the first batter, all the butterflies were gone. I was completely relaxed.

On the day I was pitching, I would go out of the dugout and watch the other team take batting practice. You'd be surprised what you could learn about the hitters watching them take batting practice. Once in a while, I could pick up something that would help me win a game.

If I was pitching well, in a good groove, and I was keeping my sinker down and away, I would get fifteen to eighteen ground-ball outs a game. The hitters would try to pull the sinker and hit easy ground balls to the infield. The other team knew that, of course, and sometimes they would change their style of hitting.

One night I was pitching against the Chicago White Sox, and when I went out to watch batting practice, I noticed something. Paul Richards was their manager at the time and he was always one of the most progressive-thinking managers around. Watching the White Sox take batting practice, I said to myself, "I'll bet Richards told them not to try to pull the ball against my sinker, to try to go with the pitch, hit it through the middle." I watched them in batting practice and all their hitters were trying to go to right field, which wasn't their normal style of hitting. That told me they were going to try to go to right field against me, so I changed my style of pitching that night and beat them throwing fastballs in and breaking balls in.

That sort of thing happened quite often. I'd see these big left-handed power hitters like Jim Gentile and Norm Cash, who had trouble hitting me, and they'd be changing their style in batting practice, just trying to meet the ball and hit it through the box. So I would use that information to my advantage and simply change my style.

I had pitched a complete game and beaten the Braves, 3–1, in the opening game of the 1957 Series, but after that I was horrible against them. I was the losing pitcher in Game Five and they ended up beating us, four games to three.

We avenged that defeat in 1958, but no thanks to me. I left in the eighth inning of the first game and we lost, 4–3, but I wasn't involved in the decision. I was the losing pitcher in Game Four. And I was knocked out in the second inning of Game Six. But we beat them in Game Seven and we were world champions once more.

The 1959 season was a disaster in more ways than one.

We won only seventy-nine games that year, the fewest wins for a Yankees team in thirty-four years, and we finished in third place, fifteen games behind the Chicago White Sox, only the second time in eleven years the Yankees had failed to win the American League pennant.

That was also the year of another chapter in the saga of Whitey Ford, Financier. It should have taught me a valuable lesson, but it didn't.

We were in Cleveland and Mickey and I got a call from Bob Feller, who told us he had a terrific investment for us and asked us to meet him in his room at the Hotel Cleveland.

We showed up and Bob introduced us to a guy named Ted Boomer from Toronto. Boomer was going to make us rich, see to it that our futures were secure. Boomer was the founder and president of the Canadian Bomb Shelter Survival Corporation. He was going to build bomb shelters in Canada and once he had finished in Canada, he was going to start building them in the United States. He wanted us to go into business with him.

The only reason we allowed ourselves to be talked into it was Bob Feller. He was very sharp in insurance and had made a lot of money in investments, and we figured if it was good enough for a sharp guy like Bob Feller, who were we to doubt it? We didn't want to miss out on a good thing and regret it later.

So Mickey and I agreed to put up $10,000 apiece. Mickey wrote out his check and left and I stayed around the hotel room for a little while. Then, just as I was leaving, Ted Boomer called me aside.

"You and Mickey now own ten thousand shares each," Ted Boomer said. "I'm going to give you another twenty-five thousand shares for nothing, if you will agree to serve on our board of directors."

I couldn't wait to see Mickey and tell him we now owned forty-five thousand shares of the Canadian Bomb Shelter Survival Corporation between us. Boomer took our checks and gave us our stock certificates right on the spot, which should have told me there was something fishy. Ted Boomer went back to Canada and cashed our checks and we never heard from him again.

Feller never said anything about the scam and we didn't mention it to him until years later. At the time it hurt too much, but after some time had passed we got over it. Nowadays when we see Bob we always ask him if he's heard from Ted Boomer. And we can all laugh about it.

I assume Bob lost money in this deal, too, and we had no reason to complain to him. We were grown men. We knew what we were doing. We had nobody to blame but ourselves.

I missed the first six weeks of the 1960 season because of a bad shoulder, and I didn't pitch well for the first half of the season. But I finished strong. I pitched very well in my last three or four starts and wound up 12–9. We also won the pennant by eight games over the Baltimore Orioles. I was sure I was going to pitch the first game of the World Series against the Pittsburgh Pirates. But Casey started Art Ditmar instead. He said he wanted to save me for the first game at Yankee Stadium, which really ticked me off. It was the only time I ever got mad at Casey.

I felt I should have started the first game, so that I could pitch three times if it became necessary. Stengel had other ideas. The Series started in Pittsburgh, and Casey had this thing about saving me for Yankee Stadium to take advantage of the big area in left field and left center, Death Valley to right-handed hitters.

Stengel started two right-handers in the first two games in

Pittsburgh, Ditmar and Bob Turley. We lost the first and won the second, and then I pitched the third game in Yankee Stadium and shut them out on four hits. But Ralph Terry lost the fourth, and Ditmar got knocked out in the second inning of Game Five; now we were going back to Pittsburgh trailing, three games to two.

I pitched the sixth game and shut them out again, a seven-hitter. I was pitching as well as I ever had, but, naturally, I was reduced to nothing more than a spectator for the seventh game.

Turley started for us against Vern Law, but neither of them lasted very long. It was one of those slugfests, the lead going back and forth. We fell behind 4–0 after two innings, then caught them and went ahead 7–4 in the eighth. They scored five in the bottom of the eighth to go ahead 9–7, and we scored two in the top of the ninth to tie it.

Then, of course, Bill Mazeroski hit that famous home run off Ralph Terry leading off the bottom of the ninth, and we had lost the Series.

The reason I was so mad at Stengel for not starting me in the first game was that I knew it cost me a chance to pitch three times in the Series. And the way I was pitching, I know I would have beaten them three times and we would have been world champs again.

But Stengel was stubborn. He didn't start me in the first game and he didn't want his pitchers working on two days' rest. He just never believed in it.

I was so annoyed at Stengel, I wouldn't talk to him on the plane ride back to New York. But in the end, Casey suffered more than I did. A couple of days after the final game, the Yankees called a press conference and announced that Stengel would not be back as manager of the Yankees in 1961, and I really felt bad about getting pissed off at him.

I feel privileged to have played for Casey Stengel, one of the great characters as well as one of the great managers of all time.

Casey was a unique individual. Except for his not pitching me until the third game of the 1960 Series, I never had any disagreements with Stengel and I thoroughly enjoyed playing for him. He was one of those managers who just sent you out there and let you play, and if you did your job you didn't have any trouble with him.

I think Casey had his favorites and I'm pretty sure Billy, Mickey, and I were among them. In later years, Billy and Casey didn't talk because I believe Billy held it against Stengel when he got traded. I really don't know what happened there, but Billy must have thought Casey could have fought for him and didn't.

Years later, Billy realized it was not Casey who got rid of him, it was George Weiss, and he patched up his differences with Casey. I'm glad they did because I know how much Billy loved Casey and what the old man thought of Billy.

The thing about Stengel is that he never showed what he felt. He was just not an emotional man. He never would hug you after a game like Tommy Lasorda does. He wouldn't fit in now the way these guys hug and kiss one another after a game.

If you pitched a particularly good game, he might come over and wink at you, but he'd rarely say anything. It wasn't that he didn't appreciate what you did, but he was kind of remote, and it must have been difficult for him to show what he felt.

Casey never went out of his way to say "Nice game" to you. I guess his approach was that you were a professional and you were being paid to do a job and you did it. If you didn't do the job, you were gone, so the fact that you were there, and he was playing you, was compliment enough.

Even when he took me out of my first World Series game in 1950 when Gene Woodling dropped the fly ball that would have been the third out, he never came to me afterward and said he was sorry he had to take me out. A guy like Ralph Houk would have said something like that. Most managers would, but not Casey. It just wasn't his way. They booed Casey that day, but he didn't care. He knew what he had to do and he did it.

Actually Casey never intimidated me as much as my teammates did, especially the older guys like Hank Bauer or Gene Woodling, or Allie Reynolds, Vic Raschi, or Eddie Lopat. I was afraid if I screwed up I was letting them down and they would say something. In that way, we policed ourselves—Stengel never did.

You probably have heard a lot about Stengel's double-talking. It was his greatest weapon whenever the reporters came around, and he would use it perfectly, especially if he didn't want to answer a question. The reporters loved it and Casey played the press like a fiddle. They would write about his double-talking and they helped build up his reputation as a character. Everybody won.

But there was no double-talking in his clubhouse meetings. You always understood every word he said, even if he didn't call you by name. Like if he had something to say to me and Billy and Mickey, he'd call the whole team together and really chew our asses.

"You three," he'd say, looking straight at us. "Don't think you're bullshitting anybody. I know what's going on and you'd just better stop it, or else."

Then, when the meeting was over, he'd wink at us, which

is why I believed we were among his favorites.

What he was doing, I think, was showing the younger guys that he would not hesitate to single out a Mickey Mantle, who was the big star, or a Whitey Ford, who was a veteran pitcher. He was using us to make his point with the younger players, and we understood that.

When he came to the mound, he would never talk much about how you pitched. He'd just come out there humming, "Do-dee-dum-dee-dum," and he never asked you if you were getting tired. He had his mind made up. Or Jim Turner had already told him, "Hey, get him out."

He wouldn't even tell you you were out of the game, he'd just put his hand out, which meant "Give me the ball," and you knew you were out of the game. There was no trying to talk him out of it either.

One time he came out to get me. He said he was bringing Johnny Kucks in. There were runners on first and third and one out and we were leading by one run and he wanted Kucks to come in because he threw a sinker ball and Stengel thought he could get a double play to end the game. He called down to the bullpen and told Darrell Johnson he wanted Kucks and Darrell thought he said "Trucks." Over the fence hopped Virgil Trucks and Stengel almost shit.

The first pitch Trucks threw, ground ball, double play, the game was over. But Casey never let the press know the wrong man came in. It's things like that that make a manager a genius.

Casey would never tell a player he was being sent out; he would let his coaches tell you. When I joined the team in the spring of 1950, I was talking with the old movie actor Joe E. Brown in the Soreno Hotel. Brown was doing a postgame television show at the time. Stengel saw us and he came over.

"You had a good year down there last year," he said,

meaning Binghamton. "I heard about you trying to call me and you wanted to get called up last year."

"That was exaggerated," I said.

"Well," he said, "you have a good chance to make this team this year. Just keep your nose clean and do a good job and you really have a good chance to make it."

It was the first time he had ever talked to me. But after I got banged around in Lakeland and they sent me out to Kansas City, it wasn't Stengel who told me, it was Turner. He said they were sending me out for more experience.

I will say this: Everything that Stengel promised, he delivered. He told Turner to tell me if I went to Kansas City and pitched well, they'd bring me back. And they did.

Stengel relied very heavily on his coaches, and he had good coaches, which was a big reason for his success. He had good coaches and good players, but that's not taking anything away from Stengel.

In many ways, he was ahead of his time. He was the first manager to start platooning, and he always was able to manipulate his players very well. Sure, it takes good coaches and good players to win, but there have been managers who have not won with good players.

I think the true measure of Stengel is his record with the Yankees—ten pennants and seven world championships in twelve years, including five straight world championships. No other manager has ever done that.

C
H
A
P
T
E
6 R

It's a funny way to look at it, but the best year I ever had in baseball started with a basketball game. It was January 1961. I had gone to Madison Square Garden to see St. John's University play the University of Kansas, and I ran into Ralph Houk there.

I went to the game because I had a lot of friends from St. John's and college basketball was very big in those days. College basketball always was more popular in New York than the pro game, at least until the New York Knicks won the NBA championship in the 1969–70 season. This game was what the smart guys like to call a "hot ticket," and I wanted to be there.

Houk was living in New Jersey at the time, but he was from Kansas and he and his wife, Betty, went to the game because of "old school ties," you might say. Ralph never went to the

University of Kansas, but he knew a lot of the people there.

A few weeks earlier, Houk had been named to succeed Casey Stengel as our manager. The Yankees had tried to make it appear that Casey was stepping down because of his age—he had just turned seventy—but the Old Man would have none of it. He kept telling everyone he had been "discharged."

It may be difficult to appreciate this in the context of baseball today, but back in those days the Yankees considered it an unsuccessful season, and something of a disgrace, if they did not win the World Series. It had taken the Pirates seven games, and extra innings in the seventh game, besides, to beat us in the 1960 Series, but we had lost the World Series and to the front office that meant a change had to be made.

Stengel's age was a factor. A lot of people thought the game had passed him by. Another factor was that Houk had been a coach for the Yankees for three years and was ready to manage in the big leagues. Several clubs had expressed an interest in him and the Yankees didn't want to let him get away.

That was fine with me. I liked playing for Stengel, but I liked Ralph, too, and respected his baseball knowledge. We had been teammates on the Yankees in my early years, and even though he never got to play much because he was behind Yogi Berra, I realized Ralph had a good baseball mind. He proved it by managing successfully in the minor leagues and, later, in his work as a Yankee coach. I believed Ralph was going to make an excellent manager and I was happy we hadn't let him get away.

I was even more convinced when I met him at that basketball game at Madison Square Garden. Ralph spotted me and came running over.

"I'm glad you're here," he said. "I was going to call you.

There's something I want to talk to you about. How would you like to pitch every fourth day this season?"

"Great," I said. I didn't even have to think it over.

Under Stengel, I had pitched every fifth day. I couldn't complain about it, because I was successful. Still, I had never won twenty games in a season because I never got enough starts: Pitching every fifth day for Casey I had won 133 games and lost only 59. But I never liked waiting four days before it was my turn to pitch. I found it boring. I enjoyed pitching. I didn't like watching.

The five-day rotation was actually the idea of Stengel's pitching coach, Jim Turner. He always believed those great pitching staffs the Cleveland Indians had in the fifties—Bob Lemon, Bob Feller, Early Wynn, and Mike Garcia—got tired in the last six weeks of the season. Turner felt you could keep a pitcher fresh by giving him the extra day of rest between starts.

When Houk was named manager, he brought in Johnny Sain as his pitching coach and Sain had a different theory about pitching. He believed it was good to throw a lot, even on the sidelines or in the bullpen between starts. He wasn't too big on pitchers running, but he was big on throwing a lot.

When he was a pitcher for the Boston Braves, Sain always pitched every fourth day. In 1948, when the Braves won the National League pennant, John led the league in starts with thirty-nine and even pitched three times in relief. One year, he and Warren Spahn pitched most of the season on two days' rest. The Braves didn't have any other dependable pitchers, so these two had to carry the load, and that's when Braves fans started the slogan "Spahn and Sain, then pray for rain."

So it was Johnny Sain who suggested to Houk that we go from a five-man rotation to a four-man one. I really could see no problem with it. I wasn't a hard thrower who relied on ninety-mile-an-hour fastballs. I was more of a control pitcher. And I never made a lot of pitches in a game anyway—about 100 to 110 for a nine-inning game. I always believed it was not the number of innings you threw that took its toll, it was the number of pitches you made.

Allow me to digress here for a moment to tell you about something that happened during the spring of 1961. It has nothing to do with me pitching on a four-day rotation, or about baseball at all, for that matter, but it remains one of my most memorable experiences.

We were playing the Braves in West Palm Beach one day and after the game, we were visited by a couple of Secret Service men. They had come to ask Yogi Berra, Mickey Mantle, Tony Kubek, and me if we would accompany them to Palm Beach to pay a visit to Joseph Kennedy, the President's father. We were only too happy to oblige.

Mr. Kennedy had suffered a stroke a few months before and his doctors thought a visit from us would be good therapy for him. It would cheer him up and it might help him in his recovery.

His stroke had left him without his speech, but when we walked in and he saw us, he started crying. He obviously recognized us right away and he was happy to see us. There was only Mr. Kennedy, his housekeeper, and his secretary in the house.

Mr. Kennedy had just had a swimming pool installed in his backyard, and it was slanted so he could walk slowly into the water for part of his physical therapy. While we were there, he got into his swimming trunks and walked down into the water to show us what he was capable of doing. He was so proud of himself and we made a big fuss over it.

We stayed about a half hour and talked baseball, although he couldn't ask any questions. Still, you could tell he was interested in what we had to say and grateful for our visit.

I had brought a dozen baseballs with me and as I was leaving, I asked Mr. Kennedy if he could have the balls signed by his son, the President. I got the balls three weeks later, all signed, but the President's handwriting was so illegible, everybody I showed the balls to couldn't make out the name.

I never had the privilege of meeting President Kennedy, although I did meet his brothers, Bobby and Ted. I can claim three presidents among the people I have met. I met President Eisenhower at a World Series game in Ebbets Field. And Joan and I have been at functions with President Nixon. He's a big baseball fan and very knowledgeable about the game. We have two letters from President Nixon that we have framed and hanging in our house. One was a letter of congratulations for making the Hall of Fame. Another was when he and his son-in-law David Eisenhower chose their all-time baseball team and he wrote me to tell me he had put me on it. I have also met President Ford. In fact, I played golf with him a few times.

One time I was playing in the annual Jackie Gleason tournament in the Inverrary section of Fort Lauderdale and President Ford was also playing in it. That night, they had an awards banquet and the President was going to make an appearance.

My friend Woody Woodbury, the comedian, a very funny man, happened to mention to me that President Ford was going to be at the banquet and wouldn't it be nice if I went over to him and introduced myself. As a joke, I told Woody, "Don't you think the high handicapper should come over and say hello to the low handicapper?"

I never meant for the remark to get back to the President,

but leave it to Woody to do just that. And wouldn't you know it, during the dinner, the President walked across the dance floor, with all eyes on him, came right up to me and Joan at our table, looked down at me, and said, "Well, what *is* your handicap?"

I was almost at a loss for words.

As long as I've gotten this far off the subject, I am reminded of another story, involving President Ford and Yogi Berra. They happened to be playing golf one day in the same foursome, and Yogi mentioned to the President that he owned this racquetball club in New Jersey.

"Do you play racquetball, Mr. President?" Yogi asked.

"Yes, I have on occasion," the President said.

With that, Yogi pulled a card out of his pocket and handed it to the President.

"Here, Mr. President," said Yog. "Just in case you're ever in New Jersey and you want to play racquetball."

The card said the bearer was entitled to play racquetball at Yogi's club, free of charge. On the other side of the card was stamped GOOD TUESDAYS ONLY.

As things turned out, you'd have to say the Houk-Sain plan to have me pitch every fourth day was a good one. I had the best year of my career. I won twenty-five and lost only four and won the American League Cy Young Award. I'm not normally a strikeout pitcher, but I struck out 209 that year, the only time I went over 200 strikeouts. I led the league in starts, thirty-nine, and in innings pitched, 283, and even though I completed only eleven games, it wasn't that I couldn't finish more. A lot of times, if we had a lead, Houk would take me out after seven innings. He figured it would make me stronger for my next start. And then there was Looey Arroyo.

SLICK

I had known Luis Enrique Arroyo in the minor leagues. He was with Columbus, a St. Louis Cardinals farm team, in 1950 when I was in Kansas City in the American Association. We pitched against one another a few times. He was a short, stocky left-hander, your basic fastball-curveball pitcher, but there didn't seem to be anything special about him. He spent six years in the minor leagues before getting to the Cardinals in 1955. But he didn't stick. He was up and down between the minor leagues and the majors like a yo-yo. He was traded to the Pittsburgh Pirates, then to the Cincinnati Reds, and in 1959, at the age of thirty-two, he was pitching for the Havana Sugar Kings, a Cincinnati farm team in the International League.

That was just about the time of the Cuban revolution, and the Cincinnati Reds, fearing for the safety of their ballplayers, moved the team to a temporary home in Jersey City.

Jersey City is just across the Hudson River from Yankee Stadium and because it was so close, the Yankees always scouted their games. Arroyo must have impressed one of our scouts because the Yankees bought his contract and he joined us late in the 1960 season. Our scouts thought he could help us as a relief pitcher.

Looey won five games for us in 1960 and saved seven, and since we won the pennant by eight games, you can clearly see what a valuable pickup he was.

In 1961, Arroyo just took command from the start of the season. He became our bullpen stopper. He won fifteen games and saved twenty-nine, tops in the American League, and he probably got most of those saves in games that I started. It got to be a standing joke whenever I pitched. Somebody would ask who was pitching and another guy would say, "Ford and Arroyo."

I really didn't mind. I didn't have to prove to anybody that I could finish what I started. I had led the American League in complete games in 1955 with eighteen. I was more interested in winning games than finishing them. Looey was having such a great year, I was glad to turn my game over to him in the eighth or ninth inning and conserve my energy for my next start. Besides, Looey was a great guy, and he had struggled so long in the minor leagues; I was thrilled with his success.

I hadn't seen Arroyo pitch since the minor leagues and when he joined us, I couldn't believe it was the same guy. He had come up with a screwball, and that made him a completely different pitcher. Nobody realized it at the time—in fact Casey was the first to say it—but Looey had more success against right-handed hitters than he did against left-handed hitters. That's because his best pitch dropped down and away from right-handers.

I don't remember teams loading their lineups with left-handed hitters against him, but they would have been better off. His screwball was so great, he embarrassed hitters at times. He'd strike them out and make them look bad, or he'd throw that scroogie and get them to hit an easy ground ball to the infield. He was awesome.

I started getting a lot of kidding from my teammates about being a seven-inning pitcher. It never bothered me because I was happy to be pitching every fourth day and I knew that was the reason I wasn't going nine. If we had had an average relief pitcher, I might have looked at it differently. But we had Arroyo and I'd always check to see how much he had pitched the days before I started. If Looey had pitched two days in a row, I'd try to finish. But if he had had a full day's rest, I wouldn't mind him picking me up for an inning or two.

I wasn't looking to bail out of there, but if Houk came to the mound and asked me how I felt, I'd try to be honest with him.

SLICK

If I was tired, I'd tell him I was tired because I knew he had Looey ready to come in.

After that season, I got an award from the New York baseball writers. In my acceptance speech, I said they should have two awards, one in English for me, another in Spanish for Looey.

CHAPTER 7

For the longest time, I thought the 1950 Yankees team was the best one I ever played on, but I have changed my mind. Now when I look back, I realize the reason I thought the 1950 team was the best is that it was my rookie year and I was slightly in awe of the great stars who surrounded me, like Joe DiMaggio, Phil Rizzuto, Tommy Henrich, and Johnny Mize.

Really, the 1961 team was better. It had everything. Maybe the only thing the 1950 team had over the 1961 team was the depth of its starting pitching—a four-man rotation of Vic Raschi, Allie Reynolds, Eddie Lopat, and Tommy Byrne that combined to win seventy games. Raschi was the big winner with twenty-one. But that team didn't have a relief pitcher like Luis Arroyo, with his fifteen wins and twenty-nine saves in 1961.

The 1961 team won 109 games; the 1950 team won 98. That 1961 team was as close to being perfect as I've ever seen, a wonderful balance of offense and defense.

It's hard to find a better infield than the one we had—Moose Skowron at first, Bobby Richardson at second, Tony Kubek at short, and the acrobatic Clete Boyer at third.

We set a major league record with 240 home runs that year, or I should say, "they" set a record. I didn't hit a home run that year. We had six players who hit 20 or more homers. We had three catchers who combined for 64 home runs, although two of them played a little in the outfield. Yogi Berra, who was coming to the end of his fabulous career and wasn't catching a lot anymore, hit 22 homers. John Blanchard, our pinch hitter deluxe, had 21 in 243 at bats. And Elston Howard also had 21 homers and a batting average of .348, second-highest in the league.

But the year 1961 in baseball will always be best remembered for the home-run derby between Roger Maris and Mickey Mantle. Every baseball fan knows that Roger hit sixty-one home runs that year, the most ever hit by a player in one season, and that Mantle hit fifty-four, and for most of the second half of the season, they were neck and neck, battling for the home-run lead and the record.

I always thought Mantle could have hit sixty-one homers that year, or more. He missed ten games and played quite a few others in severe pain. Right in the heat of the home-run race, Mickey came down with the flu. He went to a doctor for a shot and the guy must have used a dirty needle or something, because the next thing you knew, Mick developed a very bad infection in one of his buttocks.

I remember going into the trainer's room when our team physician, Dr. Sidney Gaynor, was examining Mick's rear end and I looked at the hole and I said to myself, "Oh, Christ, he won't be able to play the rest of the year."

But Mickey had more guts and desire than any player I've ever known. He came back to play, but the time he had lost cost him any chance he had to beat Maris.

At the time I was pulling for Mickey. Nothing against Roger, but I had known Mick for eleven or twelve years and we had been hanging around together for most of that time. We were very close, and we still are. I remembered how the fans used to boo Mickey all the time. By 1961, he was the big hero in New York, and I felt he was more deserving of the home-run record because he was such a great player. But, of course, the thing about any record is that whoever breaks it deserves it and you can't take anything away from Maris. He did it. He deserved it.

I liked Roger as a player from the beginning, when he was with Cleveland and Kansas City. He always played hard. And he would plow into second base with total abandon to break up a double play. He was a complete player. He could hit and he could field and throw and run. I used to say to myself, "This guy is going to be some player someday."

I never thought we had a chance to get him, but when we did I was happy to have him on our side. He was a left-handed power hitter with a natural Yankee Stadium stroke, but I never thought he would hit as many home runs as he did.

We got Maris before the 1960 season in one of these block-buster trades with Kansas City that involved seven players. Roger came with a first baseman named Kent Hadley and Joe DeMaestri, a shortstop, in exchange for Don Larsen, Marv Throneberry, Norm Siebern, and Hank Bauer.

I thought Maris was the one guy we needed, the missing link, and in his first season with us, he hit thirty-nine homers, one behind Mantle, who led the league. Maris was the league leader with 112 RBIs, and he was named the Most Valuable

Player. But that was only a sample of what was to come in 1961.

I can't remember any particular game when I thought Roger would break the record, but when he got to thirty homers after only seventy-five games, the newspapers began to speculate about him breaking Babe Ruth's record of sixty homers set in 1927.

And that's when all the bullshit started. Some old-timers began to knock Roger, saying he wasn't worthy of breaking a record held by the mighty Babe, as if he was doing something sacrilegious or unpatriotic, like spitting on the flag. Then Ford Frick, commissioner of baseball at the time, let these old-timers influence him and he got caught up in this nonsense of protecting Babe Ruth's record. That was the first year of expansion and the schedule was increased from 154 games to 162, which meant that Maris had the advantage of playing 8 more games than Ruth had. When this was pointed out to Frick, he made the absurd ruling that unless Maris broke the record within the 154-game span, his record would be notated with an asterisk.

Maris didn't know what was going on. He was only doing his job and all of a sudden he found himself the center of a storm of controversy. I really felt for Roger. He was getting sniped at by old-timers, criticized by fans, and descended upon by members of the press, hordes of them, from all over the country. He was under such pressure that late in the season, in Baltimore, his hair suddenly started falling out in patches. He visited a doctor, who said it was nothing more than a case of nerves.

Another thing that I know bothered Roger was that people tried to start a feud between him and Mickey because of the home-run race—that they didn't like one another and they were jealous of one another. And, of course, nothing was farther from the truth. Roger and Mickey were close friends. They even lived together that whole season, the two of them sharing an apartment with another teammate, Bob Cerv, in Queens, right near the Van Wyck Expressway.

People would talk about this so-called feud and Roger and Mickey never bothered to deny it; they'd just leave the ballpark together and go off with Cerv to their apartment. I used to laugh about it and so did Mick, but I know these stories upset Roger.

He had a tough time that season. And I felt for him. He just didn't seem to know how to cope with all the attention. And he couldn't understand all the criticism of him from some of the old-time players and the writers who questioned his worthiness to challenge the great Babe Ruth. There were so many reporters around asking him the same questions over and over and I don't think Roger was prepared for it. He was a country boy from a small town in North Dakota, and he had never been exposed to this sort of attention.

I remember one night there was this kid reporter from a small town in Texas. I don't think he had ever even seen a big-league game before. He was in a cluster of writers around Maris's locker, which is the way it was after every game, whether Roger hit a home run or struck out every time up.

"Would you rather bat three hundred or hit sixty-one home runs?" this guy says to Roger.

Roger just looked at him kind of funny and asked him, "Which would you rather do?"

"Hit three hundred," the guy said.

"Well," Roger said, "to each his own."

And that's the way it was almost every night.

As a result of all of this, the other players really sympathized with Roger. We all liked him anyway, because he was a terrific guy and such a great player and a good competitor, but we grew to respect him even more with all that pressure on him. And Mickey more than any of us.

It seemed the more pressure was on Maris, the closer he and Mickey became. Not that there wasn't a good-natured rivalry between them, a sense of competition. That was only natural. They both wanted to lead the league in home runs and they both wanted to break Ruth's record. This was normal and the competition brought the best out of both of them.

Then when Mantle got hurt and he knew his chances of breaking the record were over, he rooted for Roger as much as anybody.

Maris went into our one hundred and fifth-fourth game of the season with fifty-eight homers. He needed two to tie Ruth and three to break the record under Commissioner Frick's deadline. He hit one to give him fifty-nine, and I know Roger was relieved when it was over. But he had eight games left and he could still pass Ruth's sixty in a single season, even if it would mean an asterisk. Five games later, Maris hit number sixty against Jack Fisher of the Baltimore Orioles to tie Ruth. And he still had three games to go.

He didn't hit one in the next two games and he came down to the final game of the season, Sunday, October 1, against the Boston Red Sox at Yankee Stadium.

I watched that game from the Yankee bullpen in right field. All of us pitchers who weren't pitching that day went down to the bullpen because there was a story that some restaurant owner in Seattle was offering $5,000 for the baseball if Maris hit number sixty-one. Roger hit a lot of his homers into the Yankee bullpen that year, so we figured we had as good a chance as anybody to catch the ball. After all, five grand was five grand.

Tracy Stallard was pitching for the Red Sox and the game went into the bottom of the fourth inning with no score. Maris was to be the second batter up in the inning, after Kubek. In the bullpen, we all had our gloves ready. Tony made out and Roger stepped up and, from the bullpen, I could see him take that good, short, level swing and the ball sailed out to right field. Damned if it wasn't heading straight for the bullpen, and for a moment I thought I was going to have a shot at the $5,000. But it landed about fifteen or twenty feet to my left and was caught by some nineteen-year-old kid from Brooklyn.

It's amazing, but the Stadium was more than half empty that Sunday afternoon. It was a crisp, clear day. Even with so few people in the ballpark, the noise they made was enough for three times as many people. The crowd kept cheering for Maris after he had trotted home and gone into the dugout. They wanted him to come out and take a bow. That was rare in those days, not like today, when the fans bring a player out for a curtain call when he hits a home run in the third inning with his team leading by six.

They cheered for about five minutes before Roger finally came out, and when he did, it was because the other guys in the dugout practically pushed him out onto the field. Roger was so shy, he just popped his head out on the top step of the dugout, took off his cap and waved it, and then ducked right back into the dugout. The whole thing took about two seconds. Here the man had just broken the greatest and most glamorous record in baseball history and he acted like he was embarrassed.

At the time, I don't think Roger fully appreciated what he had accomplished. He was not alone. A lot of people didn't appreciate what Maris had done. In fact, there were stories that with the increased schedule and because expansion had watered down the talent in the major leagues, especially among pitchers, somebody would come along in a couple of years and break the record. Maybe even Roger himself.

But here it is, a quarter of a century later, and nobody has even come close.

It happened so fast. Two days after Roger Maris's homer, we were playing the first game of the World Series against the Cincinnati Reds. That's probably why Maris's homer didn't get the amount of attention it deserved. There was hardly any time to dwell on it with the Series starting so soon. The World Series was still the big thing and we were determined to regain the championship after having been beaten by the Pittsburgh Pirates the year before.

I pitched the first game in Yankee Stadium and beat the Reds, 2–0, on a two-hitter. Eddie Kasko singled in the first, Wally Post singled in the fifth, I walked Frank Robinson in the seventh, and that was it. I faced only thirty batters, three over the minimum, and only one runner reached second. Ellie Howard hit a home run for us in the fourth and Moose Skowron hit one in the sixth and that was all the scoring.

I had pitched two shutouts in the 1960 World Series in my only two starts, so this was my third straight World Series shutout, twenty-seven consecutive scoreless innings. What I didn't know at the time was that I was getting close to Babe Ruth's record for consecutive scoreless innings in a World Series.

It's not a record you hear talked about a lot, although it did get a little attention during the 1986 World Series. Bruce Hurst of the Boston Red Sox pitched eight shutout innings in the first game, and then, in the fifth game, he pitched seven more scoreless innings. That brought him up to fifteen consecutive scoreless innings before Tim Teufel homered off him in the eighth to break his streak.

To me, all that showed was how difficult it is to pitch thirty consecutive scoreless innings in World Series competition. People were talking about Hurst having a chance at the record and he got only halfway there. Also, there aren't too many pitchers who get into enough World Series games to even pitch thirty innings, let alone thirty consecutive scoreless innings. Hurst, for example, was pitching in his first World Series in 1986.

The Babe had pitched 29⅔ consecutive scoreless innings in the 1916 and 1918 World Series. That shows you what a great athlete Ruth really was. In 1916, pitching for the Boston Red Sox, he won twenty-three games and led the American League in earned run average with 1.75 and in shutouts with nine. The following year, he won twenty-four games, led the league with thirty-five complete games, and had six more shutouts. He was only twenty-two years old and he had already won sixty-seven games in the major leagues.

But he was such a great hitter, the Red Sox knew they had to get his bat in the lineup every day. By then, the emphasis was shifting from pitching to hitting, and the Red Sox knew they had a talent no other team could match. I understand Ruth tried pitching every fourth day and playing the outfield on the days he wasn't pitching, but it began to take its toll. If that continued, both his pitching and his hitting talents would suffer. That's when it was decided that he should give up pitching entirely.

Some old-timers I knew who had seen the Babe as a young player insist had he stuck to pitching, he would have become one of the greatest pitchers of all time. Instead, he gave up pitching and became the greatest hitter of all time.

I regret that I never got the chance to meet the Babe. I saw him once when I was a kid. It was 1944 and I was sixteen at the time, and Babe came to the Loew's theater on Steinway Street in Astoria to help in the war effort. World War II was on and if you brought two pair of your mother's nylon stockings, you got into the theater for nothing. The nylons were used for making parachutes. You could see the movie and you could also see Babe Ruth. For me, Babe was the bigger attraction.

I got my mother to give me two pair of her old nylons and off I went to the theater. Babe was there. He came onstage, gave a two-minute speech about patriotism, and that was it. It was the closest I came to meeting him.

By the time I got to the Yankees, Babe Ruth was dead. He died in 1948. I remember because I was pitching for Norfolk at the time. We were playing in Richmond, and in the middle of the game there was an announcement on the public address system that Babe Ruth had died. They stopped the game and everybody rose for a moment of silent prayer for the great man.

I don't remember anybody mentioning Ruth's record after my two shutouts in 1960, so when I walked off the mound after shutting out the Reds in Game One of the 1961 Series, I had no idea I was getting close to a record. Nobody said to keep the ball or anything.

I never kept many baseballs anyway. The only ones I'd keep were funny ones. For instance, when Mantle struck out for the one thousandth time in his career, I got the baseball and put the date, the name of the opponent, and MICKEY'S 1,000TH STRIKEOUT on it, and got Mickey to sign it. Or Mickey would do things like get a baseball and he'd take a razor and cut it all up and he'd write a date on it and then he'd write WHITEY'S 1,000TH STRIKEOUT and ask me to sign it.

We never kept any serious balls, any of the milestones we reached. Besides, whenever I did bring a baseball home, my kids would get hold of it, take it outside on the street, and throw it around, so what was the use of saving any?

It wasn't until the day after my shutout that I found out I was getting close to Ruth's record. The writers kept asking me about it, but I never thought it was too big a deal. Besides, I had other things on my mind.

Joey Jay pitched a four-hitter in the second game and the Reds beat us, 6–2, and for the first time I began to get the idea that we could lose this Series. We were going to Cincinnati for the next three games, tied one game apiece, and it looked like we were going to have to play the entire Series without Mickey Mantle.

Mickey had missed the first two games because of the abscess in his buttock. The wound was still open and it was oozing pus and blood and Mick was in a lot of pain. It was Houk's decision to keep Mickey out of the first two games, but when we lost the second game, Mickey insisted on playing in Game Three. He played, but you could see he was hurting. He went 0-for-4, and we fell behind early, but Johnny Blanchard and Roger Maris hit solo homers and we scored a run in each of the last three innings and beat them, 3–2.

Houk brought me back to pitch the fourth game, which meant that I would be ready to pitch the seventh game if there was one. That pleased me because, as you may recall, I pitched only two Series games the year before and we lost.

I went into that fourth game with 27 consecutive scoreless innings. Ruth's record was 29⅔ innings, so all I had to do was pitch 3 scoreless innings and I'd have the record.

I retired them in order in the first two innings. Now I needed only one more inning, three more outs, for the record. I got Gordon Coleman on a ground ball to second, but Darrell Johnson, my old Yankee teammate, singled to left for their first hit. Then I got Jim O'Toole to hit into a force play and Elio Chacon grounded to second, and the record was mine.

I went on to pitch two more shutout innings, extending my streak to thirty-two consecutive scoreless innings, but I had to leave the game after the fifth.

In the third inning, I fouled off two balls at bat right onto my foot. Both in the same spot. I didn't think anything of it at the time and I continued pitching, but the longer I pitched, the more it began to swell. To make it worse, I batted again in the fifth and drew a walk and had to run the bases. I came around to score and my foot was really throbbing. I managed to pitch the fifth, but when I limped off the mound, Houk said he was going to bring Jim Coates in to finish the game. We scored two in the top of the sixth to take a 4–0 lead and three more in the seventh for a 7–0 lead, and that's the way the game ended.

But in the fourth inning, Mantle had hit a single to left center and he could hardly run to first. The wound had opened up and the blood had seeped through the bandages, and through his uniform. His pants leg was covered with blood. Houk sent Hector Lopez in to run for Mantle and Mickey limped off the field.

One inning later, when I was out of the game, too, I joined Mick in the trainer's room. When I got there, Mickey was lying on the training table, his uniform and the bandages off. I took one look at his infection and I almost got sick to my stomach. There was a hole in there the size of a half dollar and it was just oozing. It was awful. All of a sudden, I wasn't thinking about the pain in my foot anymore. I don't think there's another player who would have even attempted to play in the pain that Mickey was in.

Coates finished up the shutout, which put us ahead in the

Series, three games to one. It was a good thing, too, because I doubt if Mantle could have played again that year. I don't think I could have pitched with my bad foot. Even if I had, I might not have been effective and I could even have favored the toe and hurt my arm. Yogi Berra didn't play the fifth game because of a stiff shoulder.

We won the fifth game anyway. Ralph Terry got knocked out in the third, but Bud Daley came in and pitched well to get the victory. Johnny Blanchard hit another home run. Hector Lopez, playing because Mantle and Berra couldn't, hit a homer and finished the series with seven RBIs, more than any player on either team.

Our extra men really won that Series and that's what made the 1961 team so great. We had so many good players who could come off the bench and do a job—players who would have been regulars on almost any other team.

This was certainly not my first world championship. I had been with the Yankees ten seasons and we had won five world championships, so this wasn't exactly a new experience for me. But it was the best. The end of an almost perfect year. I won twenty-five games, the most of my career. I was named winner of the American League Cy Young Award. I set a World Series record and the New York baseball writers voted me their Babe Ruth award, presented annually to the outstanding player in the World Series. What could possibly top that?

CHAPTER 8

When the 1961 season was over, Mickey and I had made a commitment to play in the first baseball players' golf tournament in Palm Springs. It was November and we had both recovered from the injuries that kept us out of most of the World Series.

We took our wives with us and we stayed with a friend, Cecil Simmons, who was a casino boss at the Desert Inn in Las Vegas.

After the tournament, Cecil invited us to go with him to Las Vegas, and we figured that would be fun, a nice treat for our wives. We flew to Vegas in Cecil's private plane, and all the way there Cecil kept saying, "Betty is going to pick us up at the airport and drive us to the hotel." It was "Betty this" and "Betty that," and we didn't even know who this Betty was.

We got to the Las Vegas airport and were waiting for our

luggage, and suddenly I looked up and walking toward us was without a doubt the most beautiful woman I had ever seen. I recognized her right away. It was Betty Grable. Mickey and I had both been in love with her since we were ten years old. *She* was the "Betty" Cecil had been talking about.

She drove us to our hotel, and the next day she and Cecil's wife cooked us a fried-chicken dinner. Imagine that. Betty Grable cooking dinner for me!

Her husband, Harry James, was there, and he had always been a big baseball fan. They were such nice people. They lived next door to Cecil on the fourth hole of the Desert Inn golf course.

Having met Betty Grable, I could now boast that I had met three of the most glamorous and beautiful women in the history of the movies.

Joan and I met Elizabeth Taylor one night in the Harwyn Club. She was there with her husband Mike Todd and Rock Hudson.

Ed Wynne introduced us and we posed for pictures with them. All the way home, I kept saying to Joan, "Isn't she beautiful?"

And Joan kept saying, "Isn't he handsome?" meaning Rock Hudson.

I met Marilyn Monroe briefly when she was married to Joe DiMaggio and she came down to spring training with him. We never socialized and I kind of left them alone because Joe always has been a private person and I didn't want to be too pushy. But Marilyn sure was gorgeous.

She and Joe had a home next door to us on Redington Beach. Joan and I would go to the beach and see them, but we never bothered them. Marilyn would always wear a white terry-cloth robe on the beach. I guess she didn't want to get sunburned.

SLICK

Harry Caray, the baseball announcer, and his wife also lived on the beach, and one day Harry's wife spotted Marilyn and she went up and down the beach letting everybody know that Marilyn Monroe was on the beach. People started coming around to gawk at her and Joan and I felt sorry for her and Joe. Eventually, there were so many people staring at them, they had to leave the beach.

The night Betty Grable cooked us the fried-chicken dinner, Mickey and I decided to take Merlyn and Joan to the casino. Rather, we took them to the bar at the casino. We figured we'd get them drunk, send them off to bed, then he and I would have some fun. Merlyn had about two screwdrivers, then excused herself and went to bed. About six hours later, Joan was still sitting at the bar with us. Mickey and I could hardly move, but Joan was still cold sober. Mickey still says she's the best drinker he's ever seen.

Finally, at about three in the morning, Joan got up from the bar, said, "Well, good night, fellas," and went off to bed.

Mickey and I were in such bad shape, our heads were practically resting on the bar. But, at last, here was our chance to have some fun.

"Let's gamble," Mickey said.

"All right," I said. "Give me fifty dollars."

I took Mickey's fifty and added a fifty of my own and went to the roulette table. Ten minutes later, I was back.

"Give me another fifty."

Ten more minutes and I was back again and we were down $200 between us.

Now Mickey said, "Let me show you how to gamble. Give me fifty dollars."

I gave him the fifty and I was sitting there alone at the bar. Mick was gone for about thirty minutes, and when he came back, he dumped a pile of bills on the bar in front of me. It came to about $1,700.

What had happened was he'd met Cecil Simmons, who took him to the blackjack table and coached him. If Mickey had 19, Cecil would look at the dealer's hole card. If the dealer had 20, Cecil would tell Mickey to hit. That's how he won all that money. It pays to have friends in high places.

When we returned from Las Vegas, there was the usual round of banquets and parties that follow the season, especially if you have just won a world championship.

Roger Maris, Ellie Howard, Mickey, and I had all been invited to the Boston sportswriters' dinner. We attended the dinner and stayed overnight at the hotel and planned to fly back the next day.

But in the morning when we woke up, there was a snowstorm and all the flights had been canceled. We waited until about six o'clock that night for the snow to stop and the airport to open, but when it didn't, we decided to rent a car and drive from Boston to New York.

We let Ellie drive because he'd drunk less than the rest of us and all the way home Mickey and I kept putting our hands in front of Ellie's eyes as he was trying to drive through the blizzard.

It took us six hours to make a drive that shouldn't take more than three or four. Ellie was going to drop me off at home, then take Roger and Mickey to New York, then drive home to New Jersey. But I talked them all into stopping off at my old neighborhood in Astoria, McCormick's bar, which Joan's father owned at the time. My brother-in-law, Tommy Slattery, was tending bar and when we walked in, the guys in the bar just couldn't believe their eyes.

There was Mickey Mantle and Elston Howard and the new home-run king, Roger Maris. The neighborhood had never seen guys like this hanging around at the bar. They were used to seeing me because I lived there most of my life, but having Ellie, Mickey, and Roger was a special treat.

We had a lot of cash in our pockets and later my brother-in-law told me that Mickey would put a $100 bill on the bar and order drinks for everybody. Then Mickey would move to the other end of the bar and put another $100 down. Roger put money on the bar and Ellie put money down, but Tommy wouldn't take their money. He just collected it and gave it to me to return to them.

Then it was 4 A.M. and time to leave. We went outside and there was a big snow drift in front of the place. Mickey was trying to climb over it to get to the car and I decided to try to tackle him. His head came down right into the snow drift, and there must have been some ice underneath the drift because he whacked his eye pretty hard.

I took them all back to my house. We got there at 6 A.M. and Joan made everybody breakfast. Ellie took the rented car back to New Jersey and Mickey and Roger waited until it was time to leave for the airport, and then my brother-in-law drove them. On the way, Mickey's eye started swelling up.

When Mickey got to Dallas, he was picked up at the airport by Merlyn, and right away she noticed the lump on his eye.

"What happened to you?" she asked.

Mickey couldn't remember. He didn't remember trying to climb the snow drift. He didn't remember me tackling him. He didn't remember hitting his eye. He thought he must have been in a fight and somebody slugged him. He had to call me the next day and I had to tell him everything that happened.

I'd like to clarify something here. It looks like all we did was drink. I especially want the young people reading this to understand that was not true. We did our share of drinking, but not as much as you might think. It just seems that most of the funny things that happened to us happened when we were drinking.

As I explained before, I was very diligent about the fact that if I was pitching, I would never stay up late or take a drink the night before I pitched. And I had a deal with my managers that the night I pitched, they knew I was going to stay out late. Not so much Casey Stengel, but Ralph Houk and Yogi Berra knew and accepted that I was going to be late. It wouldn't matter even if I did get to my room early, if I pitched a night game, I was so keyed up I couldn't fall asleep until about four in the morning anyway.

Even at home, where there was no curfew, Joan knew I wouldn't be able to sleep the night I pitched. So if she came to the game, we'd go out somewhere after the game because I wasn't going to be able to sleep.

Because 1961 had been such a fabulous year, we couldn't possibly hope to duplicate it in 1962, and we didn't. My victory total fell from 25 to 17. Roger Maris's home-run total fell from 61 to 33. Mickey Mantle, injured much of the year, tumbled from 54 homers the year before to 30. And we went from 109 wins in 1961 to 96 in 1962, but that was still good enough to win the pennant by five games over the Minnesota Twins.

Our opponents in the World Series were the Giants, now calling San Francisco their home. It was the first time since the Dodgers and Giants left New York that one of them had gotten into a World Series against us (the Dodgers had made it in 1959 against the Chicago White Sox).

Many old New York heroes were still with the Giants, but it just wasn't the same going from coast to coast as it was going from the Bronx to Manhattan.

For me, the 1962 World Series meant one thing—pitching against Willie Mays, something I wasn't looking forward to.

Willie just wore me out. I think in my career, pitching against him in World Series and All-Star games, Mays was something like 9-for-18 against me.

Coincidentally, the 1961 All-Star Game had been played in San Francisco. We played in Chicago on the Sunday before the All-Star break and Mickey and I flew right out to San Francisco after the game. Monday was a day off, and we planned to get in a day of golf and just relax.

When we got to San Francisco, I called Toots Shor, who had flown out for the game, and asked him if he knew anyone who belonged to a club where we could play golf. Toots called his friend Horace Stoneham, the owner of the Giants, and Horace called us at our hotel.

"My son Peter will pick you up at your hotel and take you to my club, the Olympic Club, and you'll be all set," Horace said.

Dutch Harrison, who used to be a pro in the New York area, was the pro at the Olympic and Joe DiMaggio was playing with Lefty O'Doul, so we felt right at home. The only problem was, we had nothing with us, no clubs, no shoes. So we went to the pro shop and ordered shoes, golf gloves, and alpaca sweaters, and we rented clubs. You couldn't pay in cash, so we figured we'd just charge the whole thing to Stoneham and pay him when we saw him. It came to $200 each.

We finished our round and had a few drinks, also charged to Stoneham, and when we got back to the hotel, there was a call from Toots. He was having a cocktail party at the Mark Hopkins Hotel and he wanted me and Mickey to join him. We had nothing else planned that night, so we accepted.

Toot's parties were always a lot of fun and this one was no exception. Tony Martin was there with his wife, Cyd Charisse, and so was Horace Stoneham.

I told Mickey, "Give me two hundred dollars."

Mickey gave me the money and I went to Horace, told him about signing his name at the club, and handed him $400.

"Hold it," Stoneham said. "I'll tell you what. If you get in the game tomorrow and you get Willie out, you don't owe me a thing. But if Willie gets a hit, then you owe me eight hundred dollars."

You know me. I'm not one to pass up a challenge, even though based on my record against Mays, I thought Stoneham should at least give me odds. Besides, I didn't even know if I was pitching in the game.

I went back to Mickey and told him the deal.

"No way," he said. "You against Mays. Nothing doing. Just give him the four hundred dollars."

Somehow I managed to talk Mickey into it. My best argument was that I didn't even know if I was pitching in the game. But sure enough, we woke up the next morning and got the paper and there was the headline:

SPAHN AND FORD STARTING PITCHERS IN ALL-STAR GAME.

I almost shit.

I started the game and I got the first two hitters out in the first inning, and then Roberto Clemente hit a double off the right-field fence. And then here comes Willie.

I really didn't know how to pitch the guy because everything I threw up there he hit and hit hard. I threw him two curveballs and he hit both of them foul about five hundred feet down the left-field line. Now I had him 0–2, and all I could think about was Mickey in center field, worrying about the $800.

I never had much luck throwing the spitball, although I had been experimenting with it on the sidelines and occasionally in a game. I never knew where it was going to go, but I figured if I ever was going to throw one, this was the perfect time. I figured I might as well try something different. I had nothing to lose. He was hitting everything I threw up there anyway.

I loaded one up and threw it. The ball was heading right at Willie, between his shoulder and his elbow and Willie thought it was going to hit him, so he jumped out of the way, and damned if the ball didn't drop down and sail right over the plate.

"Strike three," shouted Ed Runge, the home-plate umpire.

There were seventy million people watching the game on television. It was only an exhibition game and they saw our famous center fielder jumping up and down and clapping his hands as he ran in from center field.

Mays saw this and he looked at me with a funny expression. As we passed, he said, "What's that crazy bastard clapping for?"

"I'll tell you about it later," I said to Willie.

Willie must have thought Mickey was clapping because of the so-called rivalry between them, and the fans must have thought the same thing.

Actually, there was no rivalry between Mays and Mantle. Whatever there was existed in the minds of the fans and the sportswriters, who tried to build it up by comparing one with the other. As far as I could tell, that was not the way Mickey and Willie looked at it. They had a mutual respect for one another.

Mickey liked Willie as a player. I think he knew he couldn't field as well as Willie. But I never heard Mickey say anything about Mays. I did hear him talk about Hank Aaron. He used to say it was too bad Hank didn't play in New York where he would have received the recognition he deserved, because Aaron could hit for average, he could hit for power, he could steal a base.

If there was any competition between Mantle and Mays, it

was on the golf course. They were both hustlers. They were both around a six or eight handicap and they'd play against each other and they'd both start moaning as soon as they got on the golf course. Mickey wanted shots and Willie wanted shots, and they would quibble about how much they were going to play for. But they were always friendly when they met off the baseball field.

When I told Mays after the All-Star Game about the $800 bet with Stoneham, Willie just laughed.

Now it was the first game of the 1962 World Series and we were playing for real, and Willie picked right up where he left off against me. He had three hits, but we beat them, 6–2. A complete game for this left-hander.

We lost the second game, but won the third, and I pitched again in the fourth game. I held Mays to a harmless single, but I was behind, 2–0, when Ralph Houk lifted me for a pinch hitter in the sixth. We tied the score, but the Giants rallied for four in the seventh against Jim Coates and Marshall Bridges, and the Series was tied, two games apiece.

Ralph Terry won the fifth game, and we went back to San Francisco needing one victory in two games to win the Series. It rained for three days, and Game Six was played five days after Game Five.

I got the start, but the Giants beat me, 5–2, even though I held Mays to another harmless single.

Now it was tied, three games each, and it all came down to the seventh game. The rain delay gave Houk the opportunity to come back with Terry, who had led the American League with twenty-three victories during the regular season and who had won Game Five.

That seventh game was one of the best in World Series

history. It certainly was one of the best I've ever seen.

We scored in the fifth when the Giants played the infield back with runners on first and third and none out, hoping to choke off the big inning. It was the right thing to do; Tony Kubek hit into a double play, the runner scoring from third. Nobody in the ballpark figured that run would stand up, but going into the bottom of the ninth, it was still 1–0 and Terry was still pitching.

Matty Alou led off with a bunt single, but Terry struck out Felipe Alou and Chuck Hiller and Mays followed with a shot into the right-field corner. Here, Roger Maris made one of the greatest plays I've ever seen made by an outfielder in the clutch. It was why Roger was such a great all-around player and why those who watched him play every day appreciated him not only for his bat, but for his fielding as well.

Roger raced into the corner, cut the ball off, spun around, and in one motion, fired a strike to the cutoff man, second baseman Bobby Richardson. When Mays first hit the ball, we all thought it would easily score Alou to tie the game. But Maris's quick fielding held Alou at third.

Now Willie McCovey was the batter, and everybody thought Houk would go to the bullpen for a left-hander. He stayed with Terry and almost lived to regret it. McCovey hit a shot over the right-field fence, but foul. The ball must have traveled over five hundred feet. Then he hit a blistering line drive, but right at second baseman Richardson, and we had won another world championship.

C
H
A
P
T
E
R
9

If you watched the 1986 National League playoffs, you no doubt followed all the flak about Mike Scott of the Houston Astros using sandpaper to scuff up the baseball. I found this amusing because it was something I could relate to.

First let me say that I never remember hearing about any pitcher using sandpaper in my day. If they did, I never knew about it. They used other things. I know, because I was one of them. I'll tell you about that in a little while. I want to say here that I don't think Scott was cheating.

He throws that split-fingered fastball that just drops off a table. I don't think sandpaper could help that pitch. And I don't think he cheated when he threw his regular fastball, because it doesn't move, it just zooms in.

In my case, I felt I was nearing the end of my career. My slider was not as fast and I had lost a little off my fastball. I knew it, but I didn't want the hitters to know it. It was up to me to keep it from them. I had to come up with a new pitch. I decided to cheat.

I had experimented with a spitball earlier in my career, even tried it a few times in games, but I never could perfect it. Joe Page taught it to me when I was just breaking in with the Yankees.

All you do is put some saliva or Vaseline on the ball and throw it like you throw your fastball. But I had no success with it. I couldn't throw it for a strike and sometimes I would throw it and it just didn't do anything. There's no easier pitch to hit than a spitter that doesn't do anything, so I abandoned the idea of throwing the spitter for my new pitch. I had to come up with something else and I knew just the guy who could help me.

Lew Burdette had the reputation of throwing the best spitter in baseball. I was friendly with Lew, and since he was in the National League with the Milwaukee Braves, I figured he wouldn't mind helping a fellow aging pitcher come up with something that would keep him around a little longer.

I went to Lew before a game one day, took him off to the side, and told him my problem. I asked him if there was anything he could suggest. He was only too happy to help.

"I'll show you how to throw it even though I don't throw it myself," Lew said with a straight face.

I want to emphasize that I didn't begin cheating until late in my career, when I needed something to help me survive. I didn't cheat when I won the twenty-five games in 1961. I don't want anybody to get any ideas and take my Cy Young Award away. And I didn't cheat in 1963 when I won twenty-four games. Well, maybe just a little.

Burdette showed me how to apply mud to the ball so it would dip and dart. I tried it on the sidelines and I couldn't believe the movement I was able to get on the ball. This was the new pitch I was looking for. All I had to do was perfect it and figure out how to do it so it wouldn't be picked up by the umpire or the opposing players and managers.

What I did was spit in my left hand, which was perfectly legal, then pretend to rub up the ball. Also legal. But I wasn't really rubbing up the ball at all. Only one hand was moving, the hand that was dry. The hand with saliva on it was not moving, and the saliva was being transferred from the hand to the baseball while the dry hand was rotating around the ball. To the umpire behind the plate and the manager in the opposing dugout, it looked like both hands were moving, rubbing up the baseball, and that's within the rules.

Now the saliva was on the ball, and the next thing I did was reach down and pick up the resin bag with the hand that still held the baseball. As I grabbed the resin bag with my thumb and forefinger, I gently touched the baseball on the dirt on the mound. I had to make sure that the portion of the ball that was wet with saliva hit the dirt. What would happen is that the dirt would stick to the wet baseball. Now I was "loaded up" and ready to throw my "mud ball" or "dirt ball."

I threw it just like my fastball, as hard as I could. If I kept the dirt on the top when I released the pitch, the ball would have the action of a screwball. It would move away from a right-handed hitter and it would sink. It became a very effective pitch for me.

The hitter was never the wiser, because unlike the spitter, the mud ball would be rotating when it came up to the plate. A spitball comes in more like a knuckleball, with no rotation, and the bottom just drops out of it at the last moment. Since my "mud ball" had rotation on it, nobody ever suspected me of throwing a funny pitch.

If I released the ball with the mud on the bottom and threw

it with a straight overhand motion, the pitch would tail in on a right-handed batter and away from a left-handed batter. I don't know the scientific reason why this happened, except that the ball would be heavier on the side where the mud was and that would cause the ball to move.

I was never caught throwing the mud ball. Usually, by the time the ball hit the catcher's mitt, or the batter made contact, the blow would knock the mud off and it wouldn't be detected. If somebody asked the umpire to check the ball after I had "loaded" it up with mud and before I pitched, just as I was reaching up to throw it to the umpire, I would hit the ball on the side of my pants leg and the mud would come off. By the time the umpire got the ball and looked at it, all he saw was a little dirt on the baseball, which is nothing suspicious, because all baseballs are rubbed up before the game with mud taken from the banks of the Delaware River. This is supposed to be some special kind of mud. The reason the baseballs are rubbed up before the game is that otherwise they would be too slick to throw.

It's the job of the home-plate umpire to rub up the baseballs with Delaware River mud before the game. I always was tempted to tell the ump, "Hey, leave a little extra mud on there for me." But I never did.

I didn't mind supplying my own mud. It was kind of a challenge.

Once I started getting away with the mud ball, I started experimenting with other things. I guess I got bored and I needed a new challenge. I found I could get the same action on the ball by scuffing one side of it, or by nicking the baseball on one side. All of a sudden I was getting pretty sophisticated in my cheating. I figured it didn't hurt a pitcher to have more than one pitch in his repertoire. Besides, if they ever caught on to one of my tricks, I had to have another one to take its place.

I had this friend named Joe Piser. He was a plumbing contractor on Long Island and a dear friend of the family. He was also the world's greatest Yankee fan.

One day I was sitting in a bar with Joe and we got to talking and I asked him if he knew a jeweler he could trust. He said he did. I asked him if he could get his jeweler friend to make me up a ring with a rasp attached to it. I figured I could wear the ring and cut the baseball with the rasp. I told Joe exactly what I wanted and why. He said he'd see what he could do.

About two weeks later, Joe presented me with a stainless-steel ring. Welded onto the ring was a rasp, a piece about a half inch long and a quarter inch wide. It was exactly what I wanted.

Joe Piser paid $55 to have the ring made up. He told me when he told the jeweler what he wanted, the jeweler said, "Why would anybody have any use for something like this?"

"Just shut up," Joe said, "and do it. It's for a friend."

I started wearing the ring when I pitched. I would put the part of the ring with the rasp underneath my finger. On top, I covered the ring with flesh-colored Band-Aids, so you couldn't tell from a distance that I had anything on my finger.

Now it was easy to just rub the baseball against the rasp and scratch it on one side. One little nick was all it took to get the baseball to sail and dip like crazy. It was even more effective than the mud ball.

Elston Howard, my catcher, had a pretty good idea what was going on, but even he didn't know how I was doing it. Joe Pepitone, our first baseman, tried to help. One time I had the ball fixed just the way I wanted it. I threw the damnedest sinker you can imagine and the batter just barely got a piece of it and trickled it foul along the first-base line. Pepi picked up the baseball, looked at it, and tossed it to the first-base umpire.

"Here," he said, "this ball's no good. It's all scratched up."

Later, when I retired the side and returned to the dugout, I went up to Pepi.

"Listen, you jackass," I told him, "if you ever hand one of my balls to an umpire again, I'm going to hit you right in the head with it."

Once we were playing the Chicago White Sox and I was cutting baseballs with my ring, and Al Lopez, the Sox manager, started complaining to the plate umpire, Hank Soar. Lopez was a former catcher and he must have figured out what I was doing. He probably did the same thing when he was catching.

So Soar came out to the mound and said, "What have you got on your hand?"

"It's just my wedding ring, Hank," I said. "I have it covered with a Band-Aid so it doesn't reflect in the batter's eyes."

I was afraid he was going to ask to see it, so I tried to hide the cutting side as best I could.

"Well, take it off," he said.

He never asked to look at the ring, so I took it off as fast as I could and shoved the ring in my back pocket.

Later, Lopez was talking to the press about it.

"He said he was wearing his wedding ring," Lopez said sarcastically. "Well, I love my wife, too, but I always take my wedding ring off and put it in a safe place when I put on my uniform."

I think Lopez knew I was cutting the baseball with the ring, but there was nothing he could do about it if the umpires didn't do anything.

Another time, we were playing Cleveland and Alvin Dark

was their manager. I noticed any time a foul ball was hit near the Indians' dugout, it would never be thrown back into the game. What Dark was doing was gathering the baseballs as evidence. Later in the game, he had collected about six baseballs, all with scratches on them in the same place, and he showed them to the umpire. The umpires never said anything to me, but after that I cooled it for a while and didn't cut the baseball until the heat was off.

My friend Joe Piser died a few years ago and until the day he died he never told anybody about the ring he had gotten for me. He considered it our secret and he went to his grave knowing he had helped his beloved Yankees win some games, maybe even a pennant, because of his ring.

I used the ring until I retired. Until now, I have never said anything about it either.

I used to do a few other things, too, which also went undetected. Occasionally, I would quick-pitch a hitter, catch him between practice swings or when he wasn't ready. That was easy. All I did was speed up my motion or instead of going into my big, full windup, I would just get the ball, pump, and throw, and the hitter wouldn't be ready for it.

Another thing I found I could get away with and never be caught was pitching in front of the rubber. I did that a lot and nobody ever caught on. If you covered the rubber up with dirt, it was easy to do. It's just something nobody's ever looking for. When I coached first base for the Yankees, I never remember checking to see if the pitcher had his foot in contact with the rubber when he delivered the pitch. Sometimes you could stand with both feet on the rubber, get your sign, and then when you pitched, your first step could be about three feet in front of the rubber. Talk about adding a yard to your fastball.

Once in a while, a player on another team would come up to me before a game I wasn't scheduled to pitch and ask me if I was pitching in front of the rubber. I would never give him a direct answer. I'd just laugh.

To be honest, I never knew which other pitchers were cheating in my day. I just never paid any attention to it. I guess Lew Burdette did. He had that reputation and he taught me. I know Joe Page could throw a spitter because he showed it to me, but I really can't say if he used it in a game or not. He had pretty good stuff, so maybe he didn't have to cheat. Eddie Lopat liked to put pine tar on his fingers to get a better grip on the ball, but he never threw hard enough to make the ball do anything anyway.

There was talk about Don Drysdale throwing a spitter and I remember when he was accused of it what Big D said: "My mother taught me never to put my dirty fingers in my mouth."

Gaylord Perry used to deny he threw a spitball, then late in his career he wrote a book titled *Me and the Spitter.*

Our hitters used to say that John Wyatt threw a spitter and, in recent years, there has been the flak about Mike Scott sandpapering the baseball. Don Sutton has been accused of doing something. And another pitcher, Rick Honeycutt, was said to have a thumbtack on his glove, which he would supposedly use to nick the ball.

I don't think the spitball, or other illegal pitches, are as prevalent as some people say they are. I can't think of anybody I played with who I was sure threw a spitter. Tommy John has been accused of doing something, but I watched him throw on the sidelines in spring training and his ball just naturally sank. I'm sure he wasn't cheating when throwing on the sidelines.

Hitters always complain about a pitcher doctoring the baseball, especially when that pitcher makes them look bad. It kind of gives them a ready-made excuse for striking out. I suppose it went on to a certain extent, and still does, but I never concerned myself with it. I never cared what other pitchers were doing as long as I was getting away with it.

After a while, I started getting a reputation for cheating, and there was one time that my reputation came back to haunt me even though I was innocent.

When I started having problems with my circulation, I had a tough time pitching in cold weather. There was no blood circulating through my arm and, if it was cold, I would have no feeling in my fingers, and you can't pitch effectively if you have no feeling in your fingers.

Our trainer, Joe Soares, made me a little plastic water bottle, and after each inning he would refill the bottle with hot water and I'd stick it in my back pocket. And I'd hold on to the bottle between pitches. I wasn't getting any water from the bottle and there really wasn't anything illegal about it. I would just hold the bottle to help get the feeling back in my fingers before I threw a pitch.

One day we were playing the Detroit Tigers and their manager, Charlie Dressen, figured out that I had something in my back pocket. He complained to the plate umpire—it was Hank Soar that time, too—about it. So Soar came out to the mound and Dressen came out with him.

"What do you have in your back pocket?" Soar said.

I explained to him what it was and why I needed it and I showed it to him so he could see I wasn't getting any moisture from the bottle.

"Well, there's nothing wrong with that, Whitey," Soar said. "As far as I'm concerned, that's legal. But it's up to the other manager. If he says you can keep it, then you can keep it.

But if he says get rid of it, you have to get rid of it. What do you say, Charlie, can he keep it?"

"No way," Dressen said.

"Sorry, Whitey," said Soar. "The bottle has to go."

I just looked at Dressen and I said, "You no good little son of a bitch."

And Dressen walked off the mound and went back to his dugout all smug and superior because he made me get rid of the water bottle.

I felt bad later that I had cursed Charlie out. He was just doing his job, trying to help his team. Those were the last words I ever spoke to Charlie; he died a few months later. And I felt bad about cursing him out because I'd always liked him.

One spring when I was looking for new ways to cheat, I started experimenting with a concoction that was a mixture of Johnson's baby oil, turpentine, and resin. I was looking for something that would get my fingers sticky and this was it. Now that I had the formula, I had to figure out how to apply it without being too obvious. I tried putting it on a small piece of towel, but it would dry up on the towel and I wouldn't be able to use it.

One day I got this brilliant idea. I took a bottle of Ban roll-on deodorant, removed the ball, poured the deodorant out, poured my secret solution into the bottle, and replaced the ball on top. I kept the bottle in my jacket pocket, and between innings I could open the bottle in my jacket and apply the mixture with nobody seeing what I was doing.

I didn't need it on warm days, but in cold weather I needed it to get a better grip on the ball.

That season we opened against Detroit in New York in 35-degree weather and I was pitching against Frank Lary. This is it, I said to myself. I'm going to try out my new solution. So I stuck the bottle in my jacket pocket and between innings, I'd open the bottle and get my fingers, my hands, my glove, all good and sticky. I pitched nine innings that day and won the game, 5–1, and nobody even suspected what I was doing. In fact, the only one who knew about my secret was Mickey Mantle.

After the game, I walked into the clubhouse and to my locker, which was between Mickey's locker and Yogi Berra's. Then the writers came in and they crowded around my locker talking to me about my victory.

I didn't know this at the time because I was preoccupied with answering the writers' questions, but later I found out that Mickey took the bottle out of my jacket pocket and put it on the top shelf of my locker. And if you looked at it, you wouldn't think it was anything suspicious, just my deodorant.

What Mickey was doing was setting up Yogi, who had the reputation of borrowing anything from anybody. He'd come to my locker and take my comb or my tooth paste or my shaving cream or, you guessed it, my deodorant.

Nobody was talking to Yogi or paying any attention to him, so he got undressed and went and took his shower, and then he came back to my locker and grabbed my "deodorant."

Picture this: Yogi is standing there in his shorts and socks and shoes and he has reached up to my locker to get my Ban roll-on deodorant and he has put it under both arms. He puts his arms down and when he tries to raise them, he can't do it. His arms are stuck.

"What the hell?" he says.

Yogi couldn't get his arms up and he had to go to our trainer, and Joe had to cut the hair under Yogi's arms to release him. Yogi had to go back in and take another shower and he had to use alcohol to get the sticky stuff off. Nobody else in the room realized what had happened, and there was Mickey, rolling on the floor, he was laughing so much through it all.

I wonder how Yogi explained to his wife, Carmen, why he had no hair under his arms.

CHAPTER

10

In 1963, we got to play the other team that left New York, the Los Angeles (née Brooklyn) Dodgers. We won our fourth consecutive American League pennant and now we were trying to win our third straight world championship. But we ran into some of the greatest pitching I have ever seen in a four-game Series, and the Dodgers swept us.

The Dodgers used only four pitchers in the four games, starters Sandy Koufax, Don Drysdale, and Johnny Podres, and reliever Ron Perranoski. And they held us to a total of four runs and twenty-two hits for the four games.

I started the first game against Koufax in Yankee Stadium, and you know how the photographers always pose the two starting pitchers before the game? They posed me and Sandy and I told him I'd make him a bet that he wouldn't strike me out. He had struck out 306 batters during the season and in that first World Series game he set a record by striking out 15. But he didn't get me. I should mention that I batted only once and popped to Junior Gilliam at third. The next time it was my turn to bat, in the fifth, I was removed for a pinch hitter.

I always liked Koufax. I met him in Palm Springs at a golf tournament in 1960 and I really got to like him. Besides being a nice guy, Sandy was the best pitcher I ever saw. I was going to say best left-hander, but, no, he was the best pitcher. Period.

I can remember when he first came up to the Dodgers in Brooklyn, right out of college, with no minor league experience. He was so wild, he couldn't even pitch batting practice. But he developed into a great pitcher. I can't imagine anybody being better than Sandy was for about five or six years.

Who are some of the other great pitchers I've seen? Bob Gibson, especially that one year when he had an earned run average of 1.12. That's just unbelievable. And Don Drysdale rates right up there among right-handers.

Herb Score would have been one of the all-time greats if he had not gotten hurt. Before his injury, he was as good as they come. I didn't see a lot of Juan Marichal, but his record speaks for itself. The same with Warren Spahn. I didn't see a lot of him, but he had a great career. I think, though, that much of his greatness has to do with his remarkable longevity.

I hit against Bob Feller, but he was past his prime by then. Allie Reynolds, in certain games, was just overpowering. Vic Raschi was the most consistent right-hander I've seen. I used to like to watch Catfish Hunter pitch. Ron Guidry, Bob Lemon, Early Wynn, Robin Roberts, Jim Palmer, Tom Seaver—they have to be among the best I've seen.

The best young pitcher I've seen lately is Dwight Gooden. They say he had an off year in 1986, but what was he, 17-6? Some off year! I've never seen anybody that young pitch that well two years in a row. Good control. Throws hard. Good curveball.

Before the first game of the 1963 World Series, I was going over the hitters with Stan Williams, who we'd gotten from the Dodgers in a trade for Moose Skowron.

We came to Frank Howard and Williams said, "You can throw your high fastball to him."

I said to myself, "I don't have a high fastball."

Howard came up in the second inning and I threw him a high fastball anyway. It was the hardest ball that was ever hit off me. Our shortstop, Tony Kubek, said he actually jumped for the ball, that's how low it was when it passed the infield. Mantle said he came in for it. But the ball just kept taking off and it hit the speaker in center field, 457 feet away. It was hit so hard, it bounced off the speaker and caromed right back to Mantle, who was about 75 feet away from the fence. That's the reason Howard got just a double on the hit.

Frank Howard is the only batter I ever faced who I was afraid of. I'm talking about physical fear. I was afraid for my life. If he ever hit a line drive back to the box, I knew I was a dead man.

We used to play against the Dodgers in spring training, and one time I was scheduled to pitch against them in Vero Beach. I grabbed Howard before the game and told him exactly how I was going to pitch him.

"I'm going to pitch you inside," I told him. "I don't care if you hit it over those palm trees. I just don't want you hitting the ball back to me."

Don't forget, the pitcher's mound is sixty feet six inches from the batter, but when I released the ball I was only about fifty-five feet away from the plate. And Howard is six feet seven and about three hundred pounds and his arms are so long that when he made contact, he was only about fifty feet away.

Mantle would have scared me, too, if I ever pitched against him, because he hit the ball through the middle a lot and he hit with power. But Howard would take that big swing of his and when he missed the ball, he'd scare you to death.

It's a funny thing—after he came over to the American League, I had less trouble pitching to Howard. I found out later you could get him to chase bad pitches. You could practically bounce the ball up there and he would swing at it, he was such an anxious hitter. But I didn't know that when I pitched against him in the 1963 Series.

Howard's double started a four-run rally for the Dodgers; John Roseboro followed with a three-run homer off me. The wind was swirling around Yankee Stadium that day and, so help me, when Roseboro hit his drive to right field, I thought it was a foul ball. The last time I looked, it was a good four or five feet foul. I leaned down to pick up the resin bag and I heard a roar from the crowd. I couldn't figure out what had happened, until I looked up and there was Roseboro circling the bases. The wind just blew the ball into the seats in fair territory.

We lost the game, 5–2, and then Podres beat Al Downing, 4–1, and now we had to go to Los Angeles down two games to none.

Drysdale pitched the third game and beat Jim Bouton, 1–0, on a three-hitter. Then it was the fourth game and I had to pitch against Koufax again to avoid a sweep and keep us alive in the Series.

It was one of the best games I ever pitched. I gave up only

two hits, both to Frank Howard. After what happened against him in the first game, I had had another conversation with Stan Williams.

"You can throw him that big slow curve of yours," Stan said.

I tried it in the fifth inning and he hit it in the upper deck down the left-field line. Don Drysdale later told me it was the only ball he had ever seen hit fair in the upper deck in left field in Dodger Stadium. The only other hit I gave up was a broken-bat single over second by Howard in the second inning.

Mantle homered in the top of the seventh to tie it, 1–1, and we went into the bottom of the seventh. The first batter was Junior Gilliam, who hit a ground ball to Clete Boyer at third. Clete threw to first, and our first baseman, Joe Pepitone, blew it. Later, Pepi told the writers he lost the ball in the white shirts of the crowd, but what really happened is he didn't get over to the bag fast enough and he never picked up the ball. It hit off his wrist and ricocheted down the right-field line as Gilliam went to third.

Willie Davis followed with a sacrifice fly and that's how it ended, 2–1. We lost the game on an unearned run.

That's the worst I ever felt after a World Series. The games were all close, but we were embarrassed to be swept by the Dodgers. If it had happened when they were still in Brooklyn, it would have been worse. We might never have been able to live it down. The one consolation we had was that if we had to be swept by the Dodgers, at least it happened when they were three thousand miles away.

One day during that season, I had gotten a call from Tom Carvel, the ice cream man.

"Would you and Mickey like to do a commercial for Carvel ice cream?" he said.

"Yeah, sure," I replied. "How much?"

"First you contact Mantle and find out if he wants to do it," Tom said. "Then we'll talk about the price."

"Tell him we want ten thousand dollars each," Mickey said.

I called Tom back and told him that Mickey said he would do the commercial, but we had to have $10,000 each. I thought he was going to faint on the spot. But he finally agreed, and we were scheduled to film three commercials.

They were to be shot at a Catholic high school in Yonkers, where Bill Fugazy's sister was a nun. Tom Carvel had donated the television cameras and the studio and everything and, in return, he got the high school kids to shoot his commercials.

The night before we were to do the commercials, I stayed with Mickey at the St. Moritz so I wouldn't have to come all the way from Long Island to Yonkers.

"Hey," Mick said, "Billy's in town. Let's call him up and have him come over."

While we were waiting at the hotel bar for Billy to join us, I got this great idea. Billy was scouting for the Minnesota Twins at the time and I knew he wasn't making much money because I had a good idea what they paid scouts.

"We could really have some fun with Tom Carvel," I said.

"What do you mean?" Mickey asked.

"He almost died when I told him we had to have ten thousand dollars each," I said. "Let's tell him we have to have more money to take care of our consultant."

Mickey thought that was a great idea, so I went to a phone booth and called Tom and told him the deal.

"What do you mean your 'consultant'?" he said.

"We have a consultant who travels with us and he wants twenty-five hundred dollars," I said. "It's like an agent's fee."

"No way," Carvel said.

"OK, Tom, if that's the way you feel. Then Mickey and I aren't coming. You can't have us without our agent," I said, and I hung up the phone.

About an hour later, there was a phone call for me. It was Tom.

"All right, all right," he said. "How much does your agent want?"

"I told you. Twenty-five hundred."

"OK, it's a deal."

Until that point, we hadn't even said anything to Billy. Now we told him, "You're coming with us tomorrow. We're making a television commercial and you're our agent."

The next day we drove up to the school in Yonkers and the three of us walked in, and Carvel took one look at Billy and said, "Don't tell me that's your agent."

Billy never did a thing. He just sat in the sound room, watching, while we filmed the commercials with Carvel. Tom has this big, bulbous nose, and at one point, after we had done two or three takes, Billy comes out of the sound room.

"Mr. Carvel," Billy said, "as Mickey and Whitey's agent, I'd like to know one thing. Are you going to wear that fake nose during all the commercials?"

I was sure Tom would have killed him if he could.

Even though it had such a disappointing ending, the 1963 season was a good one for me personally. I had my second-best year, leading the league with twenty-four wins and only seven losses. Just to prove I could go the distance, I had thirteen complete games, pitched 269 innings, the most in the league, had 189 strikeouts, and a 2.74 earned run average. I was very satisfied personally, except for the embarrassment of the World Series sweep by the Dodgers.

Once again, I had thrived on Ralph Houk and Johnny Sain's four-day rotation. In three years, pitching every fourth day, I had won sixty-six games.

It was just about this time that Ellie Howard started calling me "The Chairman of the Board." There was a disk jockey in New York at the time named William B. Williams and he had dubbed Frank Sinatra "The Chairman of the Board." I know Ellie was a friend of Williams's, and a fan of his, and I think he just took what William B. did for Sinatra and applied it to me. If that was true, that Ellie was saying I was to pitching what Frank Sinatra was to singing, I was very flattered.

After the 1963 season, I signed the biggest contract I ever signed in all my years with the Yankees.

This was also the year that started a new era for the Yankees. We didn't know it at the time, but Houk had already begun talking to the front office about stepping down as manager after the 1963 season. Or, I should say, stepping up.

Roy Hamey, the general manager, wanted to retire to Arizona, and they asked Houk to move into the front office as our new GM. So it was Houk who negotiated my 1964 contract, which I figured was a break for me.

Did I say "negotiate"? This is how it happened.

Houk called me into his office and said, "We want to give you a twelve-thousand dollar raise."

I said, "Fine."

And that was the extent of my negotiations.

The $12,000 raise brought me up to $76,000, and that's exactly what I got every year until I retired.

A $12,000 raise for winning twenty-four games sounds like peanuts compared to what players are getting today, but remember, back then there were no agents, no arbitration, no free agency. The club had the upper hand.

Besides, I was always too easy with them. I probably could have held out and gotten another $4,000, but I just couldn't go in there and argue for another $4,000. I was never a very good negotiator. Maybe they had taken the heart out of me when I had to fight for a $3,000 raise after I got out of the army.

There was another surprise that season. Houk had hand-picked as his successor none other than my old roommate and batterymate Yogi Berra. It was a well-kept secret, but I found out about it before it was announced. One day, I got a phone call at home. It was Yog.

"I got the job," he said. "They want me to manage the club. I want you to be my pitching coach."

That took me by surprise. I told Yog I would have to think it over. Pitching and coaching at the same time? I didn't know if I could do it. I thought it over for a few days, then I finally said yes. Looking back, I think the only reason I agreed was that it was Yogi who asked me. I don't think I would have done it for anybody else. I really wanted Yogi to succeed as a manager and I thought I could help him. I always believed Yogi would be a good manager and, as I look back on it, I think he did a terrific job under difficult circumstances that year.

After I accepted the job, it occurred to me that my $12,000 raise not only was for winning twenty-four games, but for being the pitching coach, too.

We didn't realize it at the time, but the Yankees' dynasty was crumbling in 1964. Some of the guys were beginning to show their age. Mickey was hurt a lot and Roger Maris was playing with a bad hand. The guys played hard because they liked Yogi so much and, while he never got credit for it at the time, Yogi actually held the club together.

On August 17, we went to Chicago for a four-game series.

We were in third place, four games out of first, but we still had time to make up the difference. The White Sox swept us all four games and it looked like we were done.

Then something happened that I really believe helped turn our season around.

The bus was waiting outside the ballpark to take us to the airport for the next stop on our trip, Boston. I was sitting in the middle of the bus. Yogi was sitting in the front seat, where the manager usually sits. Phil Linz got on the bus carrying a harmonica.

Linz was a utility infielder and one of the free spirits on the team. He was a fun-loving guy who liked to crack jokes and, most of all, liked being a Yankee.

"Play me or keep me," Linz once was quoted by one of the sportswriters covering the team.

Linz got on the bus and he took a seat right behind me. Mantle was sitting across the aisle, opposite me. The bus was so quiet you could hear a pennant drop, out of respect for the four games we had just lost to the White Sox. All of a sudden, Linz started playing his harmonica, which was a no-no. He was trying to play "Mary Had a Little Lamb."

This was the last thing Yogi wanted to hear after being swept in a four-game series, and he turned around and mumbled something to Linz.

"What did he say?" Linz asked.

"He said to play a little louder," said Mantle, always the agitator.

So Linz started playing a little louder . . . "Mary Had a Little Lamb . . ."

That's all Yogi had to hear, pissed as he was, and he got out of his seat, came back, and said, "Stick that harmonica up your ass."

SLICK

With that, he slapped the harmonica out of Linz's hand. Yogi was yelling at Linz about not caring if we won or lost and Linz was yelling at Yogi that the harmonica hit him in the mouth and cut his lip. The harmonica had been knocked to the floor. I bent down and picked it up and put it in my pocket. Nobody ever asked me for it, so I kept it. I still have that harmonica.

It turned out to be a blessing in disguise. Yogi handled it very well. Everybody was saying the reason we were losing was that Yogi couldn't handle the club, especially the older players he had played with. They were saying he had no discipline on the club, that he wasn't tough enough to be a manager. But this incident proved he could be tough when he had to. He showed the rest of the team that he wasn't one to back off.

Neither was Yogi one to carry a grudge. He got together with Linz that night in Boston and they talked things over and patched up their differences. And everything was fine between them the next day.

We lost the first two games in Boston, to fall six games behind, but then we started to play better and slowly moved up on the leaders. On September 17, exactly one month after the "harmonica incident," we moved into first place to stay.

One of the things that helped us was that Mel Stottlemyre had been called up from our Richmond farm club just before the "harmonica incident," and Mel finished the season 9–3. We wouldn't have won the pennant without him.

As pitching coach, if we were playing a double-header and it was my turn to pitch, I would always pitch the second game so I could watch whoever was pitching the first game. If it happened to be Stottlemyre, I would kid him and tell him the reason I was taking the second game was that the other team always pitched their better pitcher in the first game and this way I would get to pitch against the easier pitcher.

One time we had a doubleheader in Cleveland, and Mel pitched the first game against Sam McDowell, who was their ace at the time.

"Who have you got?" Mel asked.

"I don't know," I said. "Some kid they just brought up from the Pacific Coast League."

"Sure," he said. "I get McDowell and you get some kid just up from the minors."

"That's the privilege of being the pitching coach," I said.

Stottlemyre won his game and the "kid" up from the minors turned out to be Luis Tiant, who beat me, 2–0 and struck out fifteen.

We won the pennant by one game over the White Sox and faced the St. Louis Cardinals in the World Series. I was the starting pitcher in Game One in St. Louis.

I pitched fairly well in the early innings. Tommy Tresh hit a two-run homer for us in the second and I ripped a single past Bill White to drive in a run in the same inning. They scored one in the first and one in the second, then we got another run in the fifth and I went into the bottom of the sixth leading, 4–2, having held them scoreless for three consecutive innings.

Ken Boyer led off with a single, then I struck out Bill White, and then the roof fell in. Mike Shannon hit a two-run homer and Tim McCarver followed with a double. Now Elston Howard threw me the baseball and I went to take it out of my glove and I suddenly didn't have the strength to grab the ball. My arm just lost all of its strength, just like that. The first thing that went through my mind was that I was having a heart attack, because I had heard that when you're having a heart attack, you get a pain in your left arm. This was more of a numbness than a pain. It had the same feeling you might get it you took a rubber ball and squeezed it until you couldn't squeeze it anymore. You arm would be weak. I had no feeling in mine.

Ellie came to the mound and asked me what was wrong.

"Ellie," I said, "if I try to throw this thing I'm not going to reach you."

I couldn't even throw a warm-up pitch. Ellie called for Yogi and the trainer and I told them I just couldn't pitch anymore, so they brought in Al Downing.

I went into the dressing room and they called for the Cardinals' doctor. I think he was convinced I was having a heart attack. Richie Guerin, the old Knicks basketball star and a good friend, was at the game, and when he saw me leaving he came into the dressing room and he also thought I was having a heart attack.

It turned out to be a circulatory problem, not a heart attack, but I was finished for the Series. I tried warming up a few days later, but I still had no strength in the arm.

I felt bad. I was the pitching coach and I had planned to pitch three games in the Series, but now most of the load was on Mel Stottlemyre, and he was only a rookie.

Mel did a great job. He beat Bob Gibson in the second game, 8–3, to even the Series. Jim Bouton won the third game, 2–1, on a tremendous, dramatic home run by Mickey Mantle off knuckleballer Barney Schultz in the bottom of the ninth.

Downing took my spot in Game Four and lost, and Gibson beat us in the fifth game to put us down three games to two. Bouton won the sixth game, but Gibson came back three days after pitching a ten-inning complete game and won the seventh game against Stottlemyre, 7–5. We had lost the World Series for the second straight year.

On the plane trip back from St. Louis, Yogi came to the back of the plane where I was sitting and said, "How about coming back as my pitching coach next year?"

"I don't mind if you want me, Yog," I said.

Three days later, Berra was fired. I think they had made up their minds in August to fire him, which was a shame. I thought he got screwed. He did a hell of a job that year.

After a few days passed, I couldn't resist. I called Yogi at home.

"You still giving me that job, Yog?"

Little did I know that the 1964 World Series would be the last one in which the Yankees would take part for twelve years, or that when I walked off the mound in the sixth inning of the first game against the Cardinals, I would never pitch in another World Series.

You kind of took it for granted around the Yankees that there was always going to be baseball in October. I had been with the Yankees for thirteen seasons and I had played in eleven World Series.

Things just seemed to fall apart after that. Everybody got old at once and then, later, in an effort to compensate, trades began breaking up the Yankees gang and the Yankee spirit—at least as I knew it.

To replace Yogi Berra as manager, the Yankees had selected Johnny Keane, ironically the manager of the St. Louis Cardinals team that had just beaten us in the World Series. There were stories in the newspapers that Keane had actually been contacted through an intermediary in August, when it looked like neither the Yankees nor the Cardinals had a chance to win the pennant. The stories said that Keane had been approached with an offer to manage the Yankees in 1965 and he accepted because he was unhappy with front-office interference in St. Louis.

I don't know if any of that was true, and I really didn't care. It was none of my business. I did know it was embarrassing to both the Yankees and the Cardinals when the two managers who had won pennants the previous year were not retained. The other thing about Keane coming to the Yankees was that he was bringing his own pitching coach with him. I was relieved. I never did feel comfortable pitching and coaching at the same time.

The Yankees started their housecleaning in 1965, and one of the first to go was Johnny Blanchard, one of the most fun-loving players on the Yankees. John was a good drinker in those days. He has since given up the booze altogether.

But despite his off-field activities, Blanchard had been a terrific player for us as a pinch hitter and a backup catcher. In three seasons, from 1961 through 1963, playing only part-time, Blanchard had hit fifty home runs in slightly more than seven hundred at bats. But John never was regarded as a good defensive catcher, or a good defensive player at any position, for that matter, and the Yankees felt he was a luxury they could no longer afford. Blanchard would have made a perfect designated hitter, but this was almost ten years before the DH came in.

One night after a game, Blanchard was called into Keane's office and told he had been traded to Kansas City for Doc Edwards, who was a much better defensive catcher.

John took the news very hard. He was one guy who loved being a Yankee. He knew his limitations and he accepted his backup role without ever complaining about not playing every day.

When he found out he would no longer be a Yankee, Blanchard burst into tears. He went to his locker and sat there, crying like a baby, his whole body wracked with sobs. He was crying so loud, it was embarrassing. He just couldn't stop.

Mantle and I went over to him to console him. We tried to find the words to make him feel better.

"Look at it this way, John," we said. "Now you'll get a chance to play."

"That's the problem," Blanchard said through his tears. "I can't play."

Of more immediate concern for me was my physical problem. Doctors had ruled out a heart attack. They were certain it was a circulatory problem. I arranged to go to Houston to be examined by Dr. Denton Cooley, the famous heart surgeon.

Dr. Cooley confirmed that it was not a heart attack. He found the blockage that was causing the problem. Evidently, it was the result of years of pitching, throwing hundreds of thousands of pitches. The human arm is simply not built to do that. As a result of the wear and tear on the inside of the artery, something got clogged in there and Mother Nature built around it to protect it. Right in the middle of that World Series game, something added to that and it just choked the blood off completely.

"I don't want to cut into your shoulder," Dr. Cooley said, "because I know you want to pitch a few more years. What I'm going to do is a sympathectomy. I'm going to cut under your armpit and go in from the side and spread the ribs, then collapse your lung. Then I'm going to put a little clip on your spine."

What that did was keep the little capillaries open all the time instead of having them open and close. And that allowed more blood to get down in my arm.

We did that, but I found I had to wait too long between pitches. Sometimes I would have to wait fifteen or twenty seconds between pitches so the blood could get down into my arm. Especially in cold weather. My arm was always ice cold and I didn't sweat on one side, which lent itself to all kinds of bad jokes.

"Whitey is the only guy who gets ten days out of a five-day deodorant pad," was one.

Another: "Whitey Ford believes in being half safe."

One night in Chicago, I was warming up for a start against the White Sox. Jim Hegan, the bullpen coach, was catching me as he always did. Jim was a quiet guy who rarely had much to say, but this time he came to me after I had completed my warm-ups and said, "What's the matter? You're not throwing good."

"Jim," I said, "I have no feeling in my fingers."

Hegan told Keane, and Johnny came to me and asked me what the problem was. I repeated to him what I had told Hegan. But he didn't say, "OK, I'll get somebody else ready," so I went out and pitched. It was really bad. I was blowing on my hand constantly. I'd have to walk off the mound to wet my fingers just to grip the ball, and the umpires were getting mad at me.

I always felt Johnny Keane thought I was jaking, that I wasn't giving him my best because he had replaced my buddy Yogi. That certainly was not true, and I actually didn't pitch that badly that season, despite my problem. I was 16–13, but everybody was having a bad year at once. Mickey was hurt and so was Roger Maris, and we finished in sixth place, twenty-five games out of first. It was the Yankees' first losing season since 1925.

I tried pitching again in 1966, but the problem got no better. I was 2–4 when I decided I couldn't continue pitching like that, so I went back to Dr. Cooley and told him, "Why don't we do the other operation?"

He did a bypass, taking a vein from my leg and hooking it

onto the front of my chest, under my arm. He simply by-passed the blockage. When I came out of the anesthesia, I looked up, and standing there next to Dr. Cooley was Johnny Keane. I really appreciated that.

Dr. Cooley took my hand and put it over the other hand. It was the first time in over a year that I had a pulse. My hand was warm. It worked out well, and he didn't even have to cut into any part of my shoulder that would affect my pitching.

Recently, I got a letter from Dr. Cooley with an article from a medical journal enclosed. It was about J. R. Richard, the former Houston Astros pitcher who had suffered a stroke.

Dr. Cooley told me the reason he was sending the article was that Richard's problem was similar to mine, except for one thing. The subclavian artery and the carotid artery join on a right-handed person, but on a left-handed person, they don't join. And that's the reason J. R. Richard had a stroke and I didn't. If J.R. had been left-handed, he would not have had a stroke. Or if I was right-handed, I would have had a stroke.

I was finished for the season, and so, too, was Johnny Keane. When the team showed no improvement in 1966, Keane was fired and Ralph Houk came down and took his old job back.

I really felt bad for Keane. I liked him a lot. He was a nice man and a good manager, but nobody could have won with that team. We were just plain lousy, and I really got mad when I heard guys bitching. A couple of them went to the front office to complain about Keane. They said he couldn't manage. But it had nothing to do with Keane. The team just got old. Mickey was on his way out. I wasn't pitching well anymore.

After the 1966 season, Maris was traded to the Cardinals for Charley Smith. Clete Boyer was traded to the Atlanta Braves for Bill Robinson. The next season, Ellie Howard was traded to Boston.

SLICK

I tried pitching in 1967, but I just couldn't cut it and now it had nothing to do with my circulation. I developed a problem with my elbow, and I couldn't pitch. I couldn't get even one inning in. I decided to quit, and everybody said, "How can you quit?" because although my record was 2–4, my earned run average was 1.64.

I could have hung on through the year and tried to fool them, but what was the use? I couldn't fool myself. I knew I couldn't pitch anymore. My elbow was burning. It was on fire when I was pitching.

It was the first week of May and I was pitching in Detroit. I was encouraged because I really felt my elbow was coming around, but when I went out on the mound, it flared up again. I really felt bad. This was the third consecutive start that I couldn't pitch.

I got through the first inning and they didn't even get a run off me, then I walked off the mound and headed right for the clubhouse. I didn't even tell Houk what I was doing. He had to get another pitcher up to replace me.

I took a shower, dressed, and left for the airport. But first, I wrote a note and left it on Houk's locker.

DEAR RALPH. I'VE HAD IT. CALL YOU WHEN I GET HOME. WHITEY.

CHAPTER 11

For some reason, I thought a class organization like the Yankees would take care of me after my eighteen years with them. They didn't. I thought they were going to pay me for the rest of the season. I guess I should have known better.

When Lee MacPhail, the general manager, told me they were going to pay me until the end of the month, I was shocked. After eighteen years, I was getting two weeks' severance pay. I couldn't believe it.

I can't blame MacPhail. I'm sure he was doing what he was told by CBS, which owned the team at the time. What did CBS care about me? They weren't around during most of my eighteen years. I'm sure if Dan Topping and Del Webb still owned the team, I would have been paid for the remainder of the season, which is what I expected.

MacPhail knew that I could have gone on the disabled list

for sixty days and then they would have had to pay me. Then I could have tried to pitch after coming off the disabled list, and if I still couldn't pitch, I could have gone on the disabled list again. I could have dragged this out for the entire season just to make sure I got paid. I didn't think it was necessary.

Instead, I did the honorable thing and quit when I knew I couldn't help the club. And they did the dishonorable thing and shit on me.

But I don't hold grudges, and when Ralph Houk asked me to be his first-base coach in 1968, I agreed. I didn't know what else I could do.

Coaching first base is the easiest job in baseball. You don't have anything to do. I think one of the reasons the first-base coach is usually also the hitting instructor is that when hitters get on first, they invariably ask the coach how they looked at bat.

Roy White would come down after he got a hit and the first thing he would say to me was, "Did I have a good swing at that ball, Whitey?"

"How the hell do I know, Roy?" I would tell him. "I had a lifetime batting average of one seventy-three."

That's when I knew I wouldn't be a good coach.

Maybe I shouldn't disparage my hitting ability. You might not know this, but Hank Aaron and I have something in common. We both hit our first major league home run off the same pitcher. Who was that pitcher? There's a trivia question for you. And the answer is: my old teammate Vic Raschi. I got him in 1955 when he was pitching for Kansas City. Aaron got him in 1954 when Vic was pitching for the Cardinals.

Between us, after our first, Hank Aaron and I would go on to hit 756 more home runs in the major leagues. I got all of them, except for 754.

One of the sad things about coaching first base was that I was witnessing, firsthand, the demise of Mickey Mantle as a ballplayer. It was sad to see him struggling to hit .240 (he would finish at .237 that season) because I knew how proud Mick was and it hurt him not to be able to help the Yankees.

He did have his moments that year, though. I remember one in particular. We were playing in Detroit and Mickey needed 1 home run to give him 535 for his career and move him past Jimmie Foxx into fourth place on the all-time home-run list. Dennis McLain was pitching for the Tigers. In addition to being a hell of a pitcher, Denny was something of a flake and a hero worshiper. As a kid, he had idolized Mickey, and he was well aware that Mick was in a position to make history. Denny decided he wanted to be part of it.

He had us beat by about six or seven runs late in the game, so he evidently figured it wouldn't hurt to give history a gentle shove.

Mickey came to bat and McLain said something to him.

"What did he say?" Mick asked catcher Bill Freehan.

"He said here comes a fastball, waist high, right over the plate."

Mickey just ignored it and sure enough, McLain threw a mediocre fastball right over the plate, waist high. Mickey couldn't believe it.

Then McLain said something else, and Mick stepped out and asked Freehan again what Denny said.

"He says he's going to throw another pitch just like the last one."

This time Mickey believed him and he looked for the pitch. It came right where McLain said it would. Mickey just crushed it into the upper deck for the five hundred and thirty-fifth home run of his career. I was coaching first base at the time and I couldn't believe what I was seeing. As Mickey rounded the bases, he kind of gave McLain a sidelong glance and nodded his thanks.

The next hitter was Joe Pepitone and, as brash as he was, Pepi figured if McLain was giving away home-run pitches, he might as well get his. He stepped into the batter's box and put his hand right over the plate, waist high, indicating that's where he wanted his pitch. McLain's first pitch knocked Pepitone on his ass.

In fairness to Mickey, and McLain, it should be pointed out that sometimes you can tell a hitter what's coming and where and he still can't hit it out of the park. That's the trick. The batter still has to make good contact, and Mick did. I'm also happy to report that Mantle did hit another home run after the one off McLain, to finish with 536 for his career. So he would have passed Foxx and moved into fourth place on the all-time list even without McLain's charity.

The worst thing about watching Mickey that year was to see him in such pain. I knew his legs were killing him, but he would never complain. Sometimes he wouldn't even want to go out, he was hurting so much.

One of those nights, I went out with our traveling secretary, Bill "Killer" Kane, for a couple of drinks after a game. As a kid, Killer suffered from polio and it left one leg skinnier than the other.

We were sitting at the bar having a drink and this guy came over. He obviously recognized me and he wanted to come and shake my hand. For some reason, I guess because it was well known that I usually hung around with Mantle, the guy thought Killer was Mickey. The guy also happened to have had more than his share of booze, which didn't help his perception very much, or his eyesight.

He was talking to us and calling Killer "Mickey," and we were not saying anything to correct him.

Then the guy looked down and Killer had his legs crossed. This guy saw Killer's skinny leg, and he just burst into tears.

"Goddamn, Mick," he said. "I was in the marines and I thought we had it tough, but you have to have more guts than anybody I ever knew. I knew your legs were bad, but I never expected anything like this. If I ever hear anybody say anything bad about you ever again, I'm gonna kick the shit outta them."

We finally got the guy settled down and we got up to say good night. We shook his hand and walked away, and when he saw Killer limp away, the guy burst into tears all over again.

I had started pitching batting practice in spring training in 1968, and my elbow felt good. I came so close to saying I should try pitching again, but I didn't do it. I would only have been kidding myself.

During the season, I would pitch batting practice a lot, especially on the road, because we didn't carry a batting-practice pitcher with us on road trips and the other coaches were older. So I was the one who would usually go out there and throw.

I was throwing curveballs and sliders with no pain and the hitters loved it, because I always could throw strikes.

Some of them even said to me, "Geez, Whitey, you're throwing better than half the guys on our pitching staff. Why don't you make a comeback?"

I did get to pitch in a game. We were playing the Mayor's Trophy exhibition game against the Mets in Shea Stadium, and before the game, Houk said to me, "Would you pitch an inning if I need you? We're a little short of pitchers."

I said sure, and in the eighth inning he sent me down to the bullpen and told me to get ready because he wanted me to pitch the ninth. I went down and warmed up and then I came in to pitch the ninth inning. But I brought my own ball with me.

Before I left the bullpen, I took the baseball and scraped it against the bullpen wall. Then when I got to the mound, I switched balls and tossed the game ball to the first baseman for infield practice and I kept my own ball.

My ball was scraped all over one side, and the first two hitters I faced were Tommie Agee and Ed Charles. I struck each of them out with three pitches. The ball just went *whoosh,* dipping and diving down and away from them. After he struck out, Charles, an old pro, just looked at me funny, but he never said a thing.

The next hitter was Eddie Kranepool, and I gave him another one that dipped and dived, and he got a piece of it and tapped it back to the mound. I tossed to first and the game was over.

I didn't know what happened to the ball, but a few minutes later I was in the dressing room and in came Dick Selma, a pitcher for the Mets. He had the scraped ball with him and he came over to me and asked me to autograph it for him.

I signed it right on the scrape.

One year of coaching first base was enough to convince me that wasn't for me. I didn't return to the Yankees in 1969, figuring it was time for me to get on with my life out of baseball.

The next six years are a blur in my mind. I floundered in a variety of projects, none of them in baseball and none of them meeting with any great success. It's a period of my life I would just as soon forget.

I got involved in a series of investments that turned bad. I was so broke that at one point I even thought about selling my house in Lake Success, Long Island. Fortunately, it never came to that, but it was touch and go there for a while.

I got involved in something called the Transnational Company, and I almost went broke. Among the things we bought was the Oakland hockey team, now defunct. I had some bad investments in real estate and my partner in those ventures took off and left me holding the bag. One of the people in Transnational was Pat Summerall, the former football player who is now a broadcaster for CBS television. We owed the bank $150,000, and I'm grateful to Pat for being a standup guy. He and I paid off the debt while the others in the company just took a powder.

During those six years, I tried to stay as close to the Yankees as I could. I used to try to go to their social functions whenever possible, or I would show up at a game every once in a while and, of course, I would always be there for Old-timers Day. I even did a little broadcasting, but nothing much.

In 1973, I was invited to the Yankees' office Christmas party at the Top of the Park restaurant in Flushing Meadow, right near Shea Stadium. They had begun renovating Yankee Stadium, and the Yankees were going to play at Shea in the 1974 and 1975 seasons. So they'd moved their offices to temporary quarters in Flushing Meadow.

I went to the party even though I didn't know too many people, except for those who had been there awhile, like Ann Mileo of the office staff, traveling secretary Killer Kane, Mike Rendine of the ticket department, and some of the grounds-keepers.

I had not even met the new owner, George Steinbrenner, who had taken over the club in January. At the party, though, his secretary, Kathy Korleski, came up to me, said hi, and said she wanted me to meet Mr. Steinbrenner. I told her I would like that very much.

Kathy introduced us, and George gave me a nice warm greeting. I must say I was very flattered. It was the first time I had ever met him, and after talking to him for about ten minutes, I really liked him. I was impressed with him. I thought to myself, "This is a guy who is very sincere about bringing the Yankees back to where they were. He really wants to put a good team in New York."

He was telling me things like, "You have to get back in the Yankees' organization. You've been away too long. You're a Yankee."

I didn't think much about it until a few weeks later, when I got a telephone call from Gabe Paul, the general manager, who asked me if I would drop by their offices when I got a chance. I did and Gabe told me they wanted me to be their pitching coach in 1974.

They happened to hit me at the right time, with all the things that had been going wrong, and I told Gabe I was interested. He offered me $25,000.

"Gabe," I said, "I can't even live on twenty-five thousand dollars."

"Yeah," he said, "but you have a chance for World Series money."

"What!" I said. "With this bunch of bums you got here? Are you kidding me?"

We finally settled on $34,000, and Gabe said the only other coach making that kind of money was Whitey Herzog.

"I don't give a shit," I said. "If you want me, that's how much I have to have."

I came back for a couple of reasons. I had been out of the

game for six years and I missed it. And because of my bad investments, I needed the money and I also needed some kind of base of operation to begin getting back on my feet. As it turned out, taking the coaching job was the best thing I ever did, because I became eligible for a raise in my pension, and I practically doubled the income from it.

I was hired as a coach even before the Yankees had a new manager to replace my old skipper Ralph Houk, who had resigned after the 1973 season. Steinbrenner had tried to hire Dick Williams, who had just won two consecutive world championships as manager of the Oakland A's. At that point Dick was fed up with Charlie Finley, the Oakland owner, and wanted to get away from him. When Steinbrenner offered Williams the Yankees' job, he accepted.

There was a hitch to the deal. Williams was still legally bound to Finley by contract and Charlie would not let him go. Eventually, Steinbrenner settled on Bill Virdon.

I talked with Virdon on the day he was introduced to the press as the Yankees' new manager, and he assured me he was looking forward to working with me. The feeling was mutual. I knew Bill from the days when he was a young outfielder in the Yankees' farm system. He had been signed for the Yankees by Tom Greenwade, the same scout who had discovered and signed Mickey Mantle for the team.

I never played with Virdon. He was in spring training with the Yankees a few times, although he never made it to New York and he never played an official game in a Yankees uniform. The Yankees traded him to St. Louis, then the Cardinals traded him to the Pittsburgh Pirates, with whom he had an outstanding career. He was an exceptional defensive center fielder and was their leadoff hitter for several years.

I played against Virdon in the 1960 World Series. After that, our paths would cross occasionally on the banquet circuit after he became the manager of the Pirates. I knew Bill, and I liked him, and I felt comfortable with him as my boss.

When he came to the Yankees, Bill brought along his own pitching coach, Mel Wright, and I wondered what they needed two pitching coaches for. Virdon and Wright had grown up together and played in the minor leagues together, and Bill had sort of made a vow that he would have Mel with him wherever he went. It was never a problem for me and it worked out. Wright stayed in the bullpen and I remained on the bench next to Virdon.

Soon after Virdon was hired, we held a staff meeting that lasted about six or eight hours. George was there, and Gabe Paul, as well as Virdon and his coaches, Mel Wright, Dick Howser, Ellie Howard, and me. We went over every player in the farm system, rating them for the future to see what we had and where we stood. It was a good meeting. I thought George was going about it in the right way in his attempt to make the Yankees a winner again. I had seen what happened when CBS had the club after buying it from Dan Topping and Del Webb; they just didn't do anything.

I liked coaching under Virdon and I enjoyed it at Shea Stadium. For one thing, it was close to home.

People have asked me if I ever wanted to be a manager and the answer is no. I could never be tough enough. Besides, I didn't know enough about baseball. I would never have known when to hit-and-run, when to steal, when to bunt. I just never paid much attention to anything about baseball except pitching. I knew a lot about pitching. But I never thought I could be a good manager.

Virdon did a terrific job that year and we surprised a lot of people. That was the year George was barred from the games when he was indicted for making illegal campaign contributions, so we didn't see him all season.

Once in a while, George would send a taped message and he would instruct it to be played for the players in the clubhouse before a game. It was a lot of this rah-rah, win-one-for-the-Gipper sort of stuff. I just had to laugh when I heard it. I wondered what Casey Stengel would have done if he had had to play a taped message.

We finally saw George on the last weekend of the season. We were in Milwaukee and we were still alive in the pennant race, so George came and sat in a box next to our dugout. He was in good spirits, slapping everybody and acting as a one-man cheerleader, and I liked that. It reaffirmed my belief that he was sincere in his desire to have a winner.

We were eliminated on the next-to-last day of the season, but George was happy with the way we played. He said to hell with his suspension and he came into the dressing room to congratulate all the players. He said he just had to be there to tell the guys how proud he was of them and to tell them he was sure that 1975 was going to be the Yankees' year.

During the 1974 season, they retired my number, 16. It was not a big deal like it is today. I was at Shea Stadium one day and Pete Sheehy, our equipment manager, said to me, "They're going to retire your number."

"What?" I said.

"Yeah," Pete said. "I got the word from upstairs. I have to order a nice new uniform so they can retire it."

I just couldn't believe it. I thought it was terrible that any numbers should be retired besides 3, 4, 5, and 7. I didn't think a pitcher should be with those guys—Babe Ruth, Lou Gehrig, Joe DiMaggio, and Mickey Mantle. All right, maybe it was right that they retired Yogi Berra's and Casey Stengel's numbers, too, but I think they're retiring too many numbers. including mine.

It's not that I didn't appreciate it. I did. I'm still the only Yankee pitcher to have had his number retired. It was a nice gesture and a great day for me.

The Yankees built it up as an Old-timers Game honoring Mickey Mantle and Whitey Ford, because that was the year we were elected to the Hall of Fame. They put our pictures on the program and they let us invite whatever Old-timers we wanted. We invited Bo Belinsky, who couldn't believe he was being invited to an Old-timers Game. I invited Bill Loes, who said it was the first time he was ever asked back to an Old-timers Game. We tried to remember everybody.

Then, at the end of the program, Mickey handed me my uniform, and that's when they announced they were retiring my number. Even though Pete had slipped, I didn't know they were going to do it that day. It was a nice surprise, and even Casey Stengel was there, and that made me proud.

Coaching wasn't half bad, a lot better than it had been the last time I did it. Maybe it was because we had a good team and were involved in a pennant race. When I agreed to come back, I wasn't sure I would want to do it again, but this time I liked it enough to come back for the 1975 season.

I never made it through the season. It was one day in May, a hot, steamy, humid day, and we had a night game, but we all came out early for extra hitting. I was pitching batting practice and I was supposed to throw for fifteen minutes and then Ellie Howard would take over. But Ellie said he had an upset stomach, so I told him not to worry, that I'd take his fifteen minutes, too.

I remember I was pitching to Lou Piniella and my second fifteen minutes was just about up, and I started getting dizzy on the mound. Piniella could tell there was something wrong. He stepped out of the cage and asked me if I was all right. Dick Howser came out and told me to stop throwing and go into the clubhouse.

I left the mound and headed for the dressing room. There's a long runway at Shea that leads from the home team's dugout to the clubhouse, and I never made it to the clubhouse. As soon as I got down the steps into the runway, I passed out. I don't know how long I lay there. A security cop found me and he called Gene Monahan, the trainer. Doc Medich, one of our pitchers, who had been going to medical school in the off-season, came over. I had pains in my chest and my arm.

I was taken to the Long Island Jewish Hospital, and they gave me a physical and kept me there for a few weeks.

After I got out of the hospital, I got a telephone call from my old teammate Bobby Brown. Dr. Bobby Brown. He was now a well-known cardiologist in Fort Worth, Texas, and he told me to come down and he would give me a thorough examination.

Bobby took a lot of tests and found that no operation was necessary. I haven't had any trouble since that one time.

While I was in the hospital in Fort Worth, I got a call from another old teammate, Eddie Lopat.

"Whatever you do," Eddie said, "don't let that guy operate on you. Not with his hands. Did you ever see him play third base?"

CHAPTER 12

After I collapsed at Shea Stadium, I knew that was it as far as my coaching career was concerned. But thanks to George Steinbrenner, I have remained close to the Yankees. I'm kind of like an unofficial employee of the team.

I still go to spring training every year and help out with the pitchers, although I must admit I don't do anything too strenuous. And I make appearances for him.

George will always say he'll go to any dinner if he thinks the cause is worthwhile. But sometimes he'll be too agreeable and he'll overbook himself. He might book two functions in the same night, or he might have scheduled himself for a function and then something else will come up unexpectedly and he can't make the function. Then he might call me and say, "Whitey, can you go to such and such for me?"

This happens about five or six times a year, and if I'm free

I'll do it for him, because the guy has always been good to me and I appreciate that.

For example, he came through for me one year when I was in Florida for spring training. We have an apartment in Fort Lauderdale, and one day I went to see a friend, Johnny Barbato, and he told me the apartment upstairs from ours was for sale. I had been looking for an apartment for my mom and Joan's mom and I always liked this particular apartment. So I went there and asked the people how much they wanted for it.

They said $25,000, "but we have to have the money right away because we need it to close on another apartment."

There was no way I could get the money from my bank in New York in time. I tried to think of somebody who could help me and the only one I could think of who was in Fort Lauderdale and who had $25,000 was George.

He was staying at the Ocean Manor Hotel, so I called him and told him I had to see him right away.

"Can you meet me in the coffee shop for a cup of coffee?"

He said sure and he came down. I told him my problem and asked if he could let me have $25,000 just until I could get the money from my bank in New York.

He just wrote out a check and I ran right over to the apartment and gave it to the people. I paid George back in two or three days, but that's the kind of guy he is.

Joan loves him. In 1978, when the Yankees won the World Series, I wasn't even with the team, but he gave World Series rings to everybody in the front office. And he took the face off some of the rings and made pendants for the women and he gave one to Joan. She loves it. She wears it all the time.

I wonder about him sometimes, when I see some of the things he says about his players. He gets on Dave Winfield all the time, and I get mad at George for that because I think Winfield always hustles. He hates to miss games and I like a guy who wants to play every day.

That's just George's nature. He does some things I get annoyed at, but it's between him and the guy he's getting on. It doesn't affect me, or my relationship with George, because it's none of my business.

There are certain guys he will never get on, which leads me to the belief that he wants to see how tough some guys are. He wants to see if they can handle the pressure.

Dan Topping and Del Webb were different. The only time you would see them was if they were calling you into the front office to fine you, or at the World Series party. George is a much more involved owner and I can't say that's all bad. I think he's often greatly misunderstood. He just wants to win so badly.

You hear so much about the other side of George Steinbrenner that I want people to know the good he does for people. He is very charity-minded. I've made appearances for him at a ranch in Florida for homeless kids that he supports and I told you about all the dinners he goes to for charity and the ones I have gone to in his place when he couldn't make it.

Invariably, when I go to one of these dinners, toward the end of the night, the master of ceremonies will say, "We want to thank George Steinbrenner for his donation of twenty thousand dollars, which he didn't want us to mention."

I remember only one time when I had a problem with George. Fidel Castro had arranged a baseball game in Cuba in 1976 and he invited George to go down. And George asked me to go with him, Gabe Paul, and a New York attorney named David LeFebvre.

We flew down, but they wouldn't allow a big jet to land at

the airport, and we circled around for about an hour before we finally got clearance, which I thought was nothing more than harassment. When we finally got there, everybody treated us just great.

The minister of sports was our host, and he showed us all around the city of Havana. We met the great boxing champion Teofilo Stevenson, and we saw the Lenin School, which, the minister of education explained, was attended by the three thousand or four thousand best students in the country. There was another school for the best athletes in the country.

Then they had the baseball game. I was sitting with George and Gabe. The stadium was packed and it was almost game time, when Castro arrived and everybody in the stadium stood up and cheered for what must have been fifteen minutes. When Castro sat down that was the signal for everybody in the stadium to sit down. An interpreter came over to me and said, "El Presidente would like you to sit with him during the game and discuss baseball with him."

I looked at George and he nodded, so I went.

I thought George and Gabe were coming with me, but apparently they weren't invited. I sat there alone with Castro for the entire game. I know he can speak English. I could tell he understood me when I talked, but he wouldn't speak to me in English; he kept talking through the interpreter. I found him to be very knowledgeable about the game, and very inquisitive about it.

Barbara Walters had been invited to make the trip, and after a few innings she came over with a camera crew and she began to interview Castro and me. Everybody in the stadium could see us being interviewed because of the bright lights.

I didn't realize it at the time, but George was pissed off. I don't know why, except that I figure it must have been because I was invited to sit with Castro and he wasn't. He must have felt slighted.

I didn't think anything about it until we were leaving the ballpark and I heard George mumbling something that sounded like, "He'd better remember who he's working for."

Then it dawned on me that George was pissed at me. I said, "Gabe, is he talking about me?"

"Yeah," Gabe whispered. "Shh! Don't worry about it."

"Tell him I said he can take his team and stick it up his ass," I said, loud enough so that George could hear.

He pretended not to hear me and Gabe almost fainted. "No, no, Whitey," Gabe said. "He'll be all right. He'll be great."

Then Gabe and I went back to the hotel. We had a drink at the bar with Barbara Walters and George came over and sat with us, and everything was fine, like nothing ever happened.

That was the one and only time I ever had even the slightest problem with George. To this day, I still go to spring training to help out every year and George still calls me to make appearances. If I ever have a problem, I wouldn't hesitate to go to him for help. And I know he would help me.

Two men were instrumental in helping me get back on my financial feet and, to both of them, I will be forever grateful. George Steinbrenner gave me a job as a coach, which enabled me to double my pension and opened the door for a lot of other opportunities. And Delvin Miller, the Hall of Fame harness driver, has been a good and loyal friend and a wonderful adviser.

I first met Delvin in 1957. Mickey Mantle was running a golf tournament for the benefit of Hodgkin's disease in Mt. Plymouth, Fla., near Orlando, and he invited a lot of sports celebrities to play. One of the people he invited was the late Billy

Haughton, another Hall of Fame harness driver. Billy brought his good friend Delvin Miller along with him.

After that, I would run into Delvin from time to time, at sports dinners or in Florida during spring training. It wasn't until several years later that we really became close friends and he had a profound influence on my life. I had developed an interest in harness racing and even owned a few horses with some people. Then, in the early seventies, Delvin invited me to go into partnership with him on a few horses.

One day, Delvin invited me to go down to his club in Bay Hills to play golf with him and Arnold Palmer. Delvin had just come back from a sale.

"Well," I said, "did you buy a new horse?"

"Yeah," he said, "I got one. Paid thirty-seven hundred dollars for him. I think I stole that son of a bitch. Don't worry, you guys are in on it."

The colt was named Spitfire Hanover, and he went on to win the Yonkers Trot and his purses came to over $100,000.

After a while Delvin called to say he had a deal to sell Spitfire Hanover to some people in Italy. I had complete faith in Delvin and his knowledge of the sport, so I told him he had my vote to do whatever he thought was best.

A couple of weeks later, the doorbell rang at my house in Lake Success. I opened it, and standing there was Joey Goldstein, the sports publicist, who does a lot of work publicizing harness racing. Joey handed me an envelope and told me he was asked by Delvin Miller to bring it.

Inside the envelope was a check for my one-third share of the sale of Spitfire Hanover. The check was for $60,000. I took it right to the bank and used the money to pay off the rest of the debts I had incurred with my bad investments.

To this day, Delvin Miller remains one of my closest friends.

I don't get to see him as often as I'd like because we both have crazy travel schedules. But we try to get together whenever we can. If he's in the New York area, he'll always call and we'll try to meet for lunch or dinner. If I'm in Pennsylvania, where he has a farm, or in Florida during the harness racing season, we'll try to get together. In the fall of 1986, we took a trip to Ireland with our wives and had a great time together.

Every year, I attend the Delvin Miller Golf Tournament on his farm in Washington, Penn. It's called "The Adios Week," named after the great standardbred, and it's a week-long binge of drinking, eating, square dances, harness races, and golf.

One year when Mickey Mantle and I went, one of our jobs was to pick up Eddie Arcaro, the great jockey, at the airport. Delvin had arranged for the three of us to room together in this big beautiful apartment he had fixed up in his barn. Eddie was still recovering from open-heart surgery he'd had a few months before. So of course we were supposed to go easy on him. Ha!

We showed up at the airport to meet Arcaro's plane and Eddie took one look at the two of us and said, "I can't hang out with you two. My doctor says no drinking, no smoking, and I have to get eight hours of sleep a night."

This was on a Wednesday. Mickey and I were scheduled to leave Saturday morning to fly to New York and play in the Yankees' annual Old-timers Game.

From the time Eddie arrived on Wednesday, until Mickey and I left on Saturday morning, I don't think I ever saw Arcaro without a drink and a cigarette in his hand. And he didn't get eight hours of sleep total in the four days. It's a wonder the guy didn't have a relapse.

When it was time for Mickey and me to leave on Saturday

morning, it was Eddie who woke us up. He was holding two bottles of Rolling Rock in his hands. That was our breakfast.

Bob Prince, the baseball announcer, Charlie Keller, the old Yankee, Mickey, and I went to the airport together. There we had a few more drinks at the bar. Then we got on the plane and flew to New York.

We got to the stadium about an hour before the Old-timers ceremonies. I was half in the bag. Mickey was just as bad. But for some reason, I had committed myself to pitch in the game that year and Mick had agreed to play also.

I went to the mound and I was worried about throwing strikes. My aim was not too good because I was having trouble seeing. Mickey was batting and I knew he liked the ball up and in batting right-handed. I tried to throw it there, but from the shape I was in, I couldn't guarantee where the ball was going to go. I got the ball a little inside and Mickey pulled it foul along the third-base line.

Then he motioned for me to get it out over the plate a little and, amazingly, the next pitch was exactly where he wanted it. Mickey got into it and drove a shot into the bullpen. There were sixty thousand people in the stadium and they just went wild. That was the most noise I ever heard standing on the mound in Yankee Stadium.

Now I knew what opposing pitchers used to hear when Mickey or Roger Maris hit a home run off them in front of a big crowd at Yankee Stadium.

The Hall of Fame induction ceremonies in Cooperstown, N.Y., were scheduled for Sunday, August 11, 1974. We were on a West Coast trip at the time, and I made part of the trip, then left after a Friday game in Anaheim and flew all night to New York. Joan picked me up at the airport and we drove up to Cooperstown, to the Otesaga Hotel.

Sally Ann and her husband, Steve, came with us, and so did Tommy. Eddie was playing for the Red Sox farm team in Niagara Falls and his plan was to drive over to Cooperstown after playing a game on Saturday night. That way he could be there for the Sunday ceremonies.

Mickey had rented a bus and a lot of my friends and family went up on it.

I was nervous all the way up, worrying about the speech I had to make.

The best part of the weekend is a private dinner they have on Saturday night just for the commissioner and members of the Hall of Fame. No press, no guests—just the recent inductees and whatever Hall of Famers accept the invitation to come back for the induction ceremonies. It's at this dinner that you are presented with the Hall of Fame ring.

Joe DiMaggio was there and Casey Stengel, Hank Greenberg, Satchel Paige, Charlie Gehringer, and Bill Terry. We just sat around telling stories and having dinner and I had a great time, until Commissioner Kuhn asked me to get up and say a few words. I never expected that and I wasn't prepared, but somehow I got through it.

After dinner, I went to my room to work on my speech for the next day. I couldn't believe it when Mickey told me he wasn't even going to prepare a speech.

"You're crazy, Mick," I said. "I'm telling you, you'd better write something down or you're going to be lost for words when you get up there."

Mickey just waved me off and went to play pool with his four sons, Mickey, Danny, David, and Billy, and my son Tommy. They stayed up practically all night shooting pool and drinking beer, and the next day he made his speech off the cuff. He never wrote down a word and I was nervous for him, but he was great.

He had the crowd in stitches. One of the things he talked about was all the bad investments he made, including a chain of Mickey Mantle chicken restaurants.

"Our slogan was 'To get a better piece of chicken, you have to be a rooster,'" Mickey said, and it just broke everybody up. Mick's wife, Merlyn, still gets embarrassed when you remind her of that line.

My son Eddie drove all night from Niagara Falls and arrived at 5 A.M., but they wouldn't believe he was Eddie Ford, so he wound up sleeping in the lobby.

Steve and Eleanor Clancy, my daughter's in-laws, said they hardly slept all night either, because they had the bad luck to be in the room right next to Casey Stengel, and he kept them up all night talking. The walls were very thin and they could hear every word he was saying.

Casey had been up late with us drinking and he was eighty-four at the time and a little out of it, so when he got to his room, he was talking nonstop. The Clancys couldn't make out exactly what he was saying, but they said it sounded like he was arguing with an umpire. At first they thought he was talking in his sleep, but then they realized he was wide awake. Then they wondered who was in the room with him. But they heard only his voice. It turned out Casey was rooming alone.

And, of course, I stayed up almost all night trying to write a speech and having a tough time finding the right things to say.

Finally, it was time for the ceremonies. We were all sitting on this veranda outside the library in Cooperstown, the Hall of Famers and the four inductees: umpire Jocko Conlan, Cool Papa Bell, an old star from the Negro Leagues, Mickey, and me. Commissioner Kuhn served as the master of ceremonies. He would call each of us up, read what was engraved on our plaques, present us with a facsimile of the plaque, then sit down while each of us inductees made his speech.

Cool Papa Bell went first, and when it was time for him to speak, he introduced everybody he knew in the audience. He introduced his family, his cousins, his second cousins, his third cousins. He introduced his third-grade teacher. He must have introduced twenty-five people. But he forgot one. His wife. She was ready to kill him after the ceremonies.

Jocko Conlan was second. He made a nice speech and then he sat down, right next to me. I hardly was paying any attention to him, I was so worried about my speech. Now, it was just about twenty seconds before Kuhn was supposed to introduce me, and Jocko grabbed my arm and said, "I'm getting pains in my chest."

"Oh, God," I thought to myself. "The man's going to have a heart attack right here on the stage."

I was really shaken up. Jocko was seventy-five at the time and I was thinking, "Oh, Christ, poor Jocko's going to die right up here."

But he was all right. It turned out it was just the heat and the excitement of the day. It's thirteen years later and Jocko is still going.

I really didn't make a very good speech. I introduced the members of my family, and remembered to include Joan, and I thanked my teammates and the Yankees. I had one line that got a reaction. Gerald Ford had become President that week and I said, "This is a great week for the Fords."

And it was. At least it was for this Ford.

I have been retired from the game for twenty years now, but you're not going to get this old-timer to knock the game as it is today, or today's players for that matter.

Sure, the game has its problems, but it always has had some problems.

As far as today's players, I think individually they are just as good, if not better, than we were thirty years ago. The talent is diluted because there are 250 more players in the major leagues now than there were back then. That's enough for a whole minor league, ten teams. If we were back to sixteen, the teams would be every bit as good as they were in my day.

One thing that hurts today is that there are fewer minor league teams. That means the players don't get the instruction we used to get and they don't hang around in the minor leagues like we used to. If they don't make it in two or three years, they get out, and I can't blame them.

I know this: Hitting is tougher than it was in my day. The pitchers are bigger and stronger now and they have more pitches. When I came up, it was a fastball, a curve, and a change-up. Now, it's a slider, two or three different kinds of fastballs—you have the split-fingered fastball.

Also you have better relief pitchers today. There were good relief pitchers in my day, too, but now on most teams the relief pitcher is the best pitcher on the team. That's changed since I was playing. Every team has a relief pitcher who throws the ball ninety miles an hour or better. These days, they train a kid to be a relief pitcher in college or from the time he becomes a minor leaguer. They never did that in my day.

If there is one disappointment I have about baseball these days it's that there are only two teams in New York and they have never enjoyed success in the same year. Back when I was playing, we had three teams in New York. It was so exciting then, and such a great area to grow up in if you were a sports fan.

The 1986 Mets showed how New York can go crazy over a baseball team. It made me fantasize about what it would be like if the Yankees and Mets ever met in a World Series. I hope that doesn't offend people from other cities, but the truth is, once a Yankee, always a Yankee.

I also mentioned earlier that the one real regret I have in my life is that I never attended college. If I had it to do over again, I would. And I urge all young people to compete in sports, *and* stay in school.

We can't all be major league baseball players. I was one of the fortunate few. It has been a great life, especially because I was able to do the thing I loved to do best—play baseball—and do it for a living. You can't be luckier than that.

I loved what I did—I think I did it well, and I hope I have given back something to the game that has been so good to me.

The highlight, of course, was making the Hall of Fame. It was a day I will never forget, especially since I was able to go in together with my closest buddy, Mickey Mantle.

After the ceremonies in Cooperstown, Stengel was asked by the photographers to pose for a picture with Mickey and me. Casey never congratulated us for getting in the Hall of Fame. He didn't have to. When the photographers asked him to pose with Mickey and me with our plaques, you could just see by the look in his eyes how proud he was that we both got in. He would never say so because that just wasn't his way, but you could tell.

I was just as proud. Here I was, a kid off the streets of New York, with a plaque hanging in the Baseball Hall of Fame. And I knew that was something that could never be taken away from me. It would be there forever.

INDEX

Index

Index

Index

Index

Index